Unbreákable Love

The Love of God in the Message of the Prophets

To Ruth
— a mother in Israel —
with love from
us both.
Cliff & Monica

Clifford Hill

This version is produced by:

Centre for Contemporary Ministry
Moggerhanger Park, Bedford MK44 3RW
United Kingdom

Distributed by: C & M Ministries Trust of the same address.

Final UK Editing by Monica Hill for Centre for Contemporary Ministry

Graphic design Edenic Media.

British Library Cataloguing in Publication Data:

A catalogue record for this publication is available from the British Library.

ISBN: 978-0-9533429-8-3

First Edition

Printed in the United Kingdom by EuropaPrint
for Centre for Contemporary Ministry 2010.

Contents

The Prologue examines the need for an understanding of the true love of God. This is seen against the background of the great shaking of the nations which is taking place today, including the worldwide financial crisis that began in 2008 and the volcanic ash that closed air traffic over Europe in 2010. It reports a dramatic rescue in the Swiss Alps illustrating God's self-sacrificial love.

Chapter One

This chapter deals with the message God sent to his people in exile in Babylon in response to their cries for help as they felt unloved and unwanted. The message shows God's tender loving care for those who are oppressed and who have nothing to offer in return for his love.

Chapter Two

The Prophet Hosea had a turbulent marriage but his unbreakable love for his unfaithful wife won her love in the end. From this Hosea learned a unique message about the unbreakable love of God.

Chapter Three

This chapter has messages from both Isaiah and Jeremiah that reveal the amazing power of the unbreakable love of God to dispel depression, drive out bitterness and set people free from despair.

Chapter Four

This chapter examines the way the Prophets discovered the unbreakable love of God, his special love for the weak and powerless, and how his love builds them up and strengthens them, transforming their lives.

This chapter traces the Hebraic roots of the 'Fatherhood of God' which is central to the New Testament and the teaching of Jesus. It shows the reason why God is not referred to as Father in the Old Testament until after the return from exile in Babylon.

This chapter examines how the love of God has acted to break the power of human sin and to bring us into a right relationship with himself. It unpacks the Hebraic background to Paul's teaching on the law, grace and the atonement with special mention of the rabbinic teaching on the 'Second Adam' and the Messianic mission to transform the whole natural order of creation.

This chapter offers a brief summary of the message of the prophets which revealed the nature of God as 'Unbreakable Love'. It shows how the Hebraic background to the New Testament was lost soon after the Apostolic Age and at the Council of Nicaea no one could speak Hebrew and the church lost its roots, with the result that the revelation of the nature of God and his unbreakable love brought through the prophets was lost. It was not recovered in the Reformation and the chapter ends with a plea for a new biblically based Reformation.

ACKNOWLEDGEMENTS

I am very grateful to the trustees of both **C & M Ministries** and the **Centre for Contemporary Ministry** who have not only encouraged me in pursuing the study that has led to this book but several of them have taken the time to read the manuscript and make helpful comments. I am particularly grateful to the Revd Roger Whitehead, chairman of the CCM trustees, the Revd Gillian Orpin, John Robins, Paul Cadywould, Philip Kelly, Dorothy Horsman and Teresa Britton for their tireless proof-reading.

I am especially indebted to The Rt Revd Dr John Taylor, former Bishop of St Albans, for reading part of the manuscript and giving me the benefit of his considerable Old Testament scholarship. The Revd Dr Derek Moore-Crispin, Dr Robert Rowe and Ken Wallace also offered a number of useful critical comments on the draft manuscript and I am most grateful to them.

Most of all I am grateful to Monica, my wife, for support throughout the writing of this book and practical help in numerous ways including generating the index, arranging proof-readers and overall editing.

Unbreakable *Love*

The Love of God in the Message of the Prophets

Clifford Hill

Chapters One - Nine

each look at a different part of the love of God that was discovered by the prophets.

_____

Chapters Ten -Twelve

explore new depths in the truths revealed by the prophets and link them with the life and teaching of Jesus.

_____

Before starting on an exciting journey of discovery...

make sure you read the Prologue!

INTRODUCTION

How can we learn about God?
What is he really like?

Long before the birth of Jesus the Prophets of Israel made some life-changing discoveries about the nature of God.

The Prophets found that God was not only a God of justice but also of mercy, compassion and love! They found that God was patient and forgiving; that he was faithful, reliable, always keeping his promises. They found that God longed to bless people and to embrace them in his love.

They also learned that God had made human beings in his own image so that our humanity at its best is a reflection of the nature of God.

But the life and work of the prophets of Israel that form a large part of what we know as the Old Testament in the Bible rarely features in the teaching of the Western churches today. Consequently the message of the prophets is unknown to a large majority of Christians. Yet this message is foundational to the New Testament and to the ministry and mission of Jesus and the Apostles.

Without an understanding of the nature and purposes of God revealed through the prophets of Israel we cannot gain a full understanding of what is revealed in the New Testament.

The message of the prophets brings the Bible alive in a new way!

How did the prophets discover so much about the nature and purposes of God? How did they learn, like Jeremiah, to stand in the 'Council of the Lord' and to get into the 'secret place of the Most High'?

How did the prophets discover the unbreakable love of God that prepared the way for the coming of Jesus?

That's what this book is all about. The book is written for Christians and non-Christians. Both will find it informative and challenging.

PROLOGUE

The Prologue examines the need for an understanding of the true love of God. This is seen against the background of the great shaking of the nations which is taking place today, including the worldwide financial crisis that began in 2008 and the volcanic ash that closed air traffic over Europe in 2010. It reports a dramatic rescue in the Swiss Alps illustrating God's self-sacrificial love.

Everyone Needs Love

All human beings need love. The most popular books are love stories. From the earliest moments of childhood the new-born baby craves the comfort and security of contact with the mother, long before the child is able to identify this as a response to love. As the child grows, the demand for love grows. The mature adult recognises that love is a two-way process of giving and receiving. Sadly, many adults do not reach this level of maturity in their emotional *persona* and their demand for love is stronger than the ability to give love. This is often the outcome of being starved of love in childhood or of psychological damage due to suffering a broken home at a vulnerable age.

A Marriage of Love

This was brought home to me dramatically when a young couple came to me asking to be married. As always I gently led them to talk about their circumstances so that I could exercise some pastoral ministry and prepare them for marriage. They were both in professional jobs, in their mid-20s, and had been living together for nearly a year. When we had sufficiently established a relationship I asked directly why they wanted to get married and after a few moments silence the bride-to-be broke down and wept.

Between tears she poured out a tale of family breakdown. Her father had left home when she was a baby leaving her mother with two small children. Both her mother and her father had gone from one relationship to another which had had an unsettling effect upon her childhood and teenage years from which she was still suffering.

The bridegroom also had a history of family breakdown. He told his story with difficulty and suppressed emotion. Eventually they both looked up and said, "We don't want that! We want something different."

Opening my Bible I said, "I want to read something to you of what God says about love". I read a few verses from 1 Corinthians 13.

"Love is patient, love is kind. It does not envy, it does not boast, it is not proud. It is not rude, it is not self-seeking, it is not easily angered, it keeps no record of wrongs. Love does not delight in evil but rejoices with the truth. It always protects, always trusts, always hopes, always perseveres. Love never fails"

"That's what we want" they both said.

It led easily into a discussion of the nature of love and I was able to say that the most fulfilling love relationship is where there is mutual giving and receiving; where the objective of each one is to give joy and happiness to the other so that their receiving becomes a by-product of giving. If each of the partners in a relationship is more concerned for the well-being of the other than their own happiness there will be a relationship of mutual love. That's what the Apostle Paul was beautifully expressing in his letter to the Christians in Corinth. I then went on to talk about the source of this kind of love, saying that God loves us with an unending love and that when we gain a personal experience of his love it transforms our own love relationships.

This young couple went on to have a lovely wedding service and reception with the different branches of their complex families coming together, resulting in some reconciliation and healing of relationships that had been broken for many years. It was the witness of the couple themselves that spoke powerfully to some of their relatives who could see the change in them. They had been attending church for about three months prior to the wedding although neither had any previous church background.

On their first Sunday morning after attending church they reported to me afterwards that they enjoyed the talk but they couldn't get on with all that singing! Of course, worship was entirely foreign to them as they didn't know God. You can't express the 'worth-ship' of someone you don't know. But slowly the love of Jesus began working within them and it was not long before each of them became Christians. Their wedding was a particularly joyful occasion, much to the joy of their new-found friends.

Broken Families

Their story has a happy ending because they were able to reach out beyond themselves, recognising that they needed help, and it wasn't long before God began to break down barriers of past experience within each of them so that they could respond to his love. The transformative power of God's love had brought about a total change in their lives: they had discovered the kind of love that the Apostle Paul described.

It is tragically true that the major reason for the high rate of family breakdown today throughout the Western nations is the failure to understand this love which Paul describes that is not self-seeking or easily angered and keeps no record of wrongs. Sadly, the environment in which many children are brought up today is not one of protective love but of exposure to the often violent quarrels of the two adults who are most important in their lives. All too often the young parents are themselves the product of a broken home. The facts show that divorce and relationship breakdown recur from one generation to the next. Those whose parents have broken up are twice as likely to suffer a broken relationship as those who grow up in intact families.

In the summer of 2009 the media in Britain began using the term 'Broken Britain' which was a reflection of the increasing public awareness of the wide range of social, economic and health problems that can be traced to the breakdown of family life. This growing recognition that there is something seriously wrong in the life of the nation was linked with incidents such as the two boys aged 10 and 11 who deliberately tortured two other children.

The two boys were living in a former mining village outside Doncaster when they lured two other boys aged 9 and 11 onto a piece of waste ground and then robbed them, beat them, burned them with cigarettes and sexually humiliated them leaving one of them unconscious and half submerged in water. He had been smashed on the head with a broken sink and left for dead.

The whole nation was stunned that two children could be so cruel and evil. But these boys came from a highly dysfunctional family. They had a violent drunken father who beat them and made them fight each other, and an equally drunken, drug-addicted mother. She had no control over her seven sons - born to 3 different men. She put up a sign outside her house in Doncaster that said "BEWARE OF THE KIDS" and she made no attempt to stop them terrorising other children and families in the neighbourhood. She didn't even feed them adequately and they were often seen scavenging from refuse bins. When she was told of her sons' arrest she shouted, "It's now't to do with me!" She had already washed her hands of the two boys because a month earlier they had been taken from her by social workers and placed with foster parents, an elderly couple who were quite unable to cope with them. Nothing could be more clear than that these two little boys had never known the love and security of a stable home life.

Children Starved of Love

This incident was widely discussed in the media. Writing in the *Daily Mail*, Melanie Phillips said that this atrocity was a symptom of the social and cultural crisis in Britain today. She said that there are thousands of other children being raised in similar backgrounds. Iain Duncan Smith, writing in the *Daily Telegraph* advocated taking both mother and child from dysfunctional families into care which he believed would be cheaper than the state having to deal with children who come from disturbed and violent homes who will spend the whole of their lives on benefits or in prison. It would not be unreasonable to doubt whether this will be any more effective than the present policy of taking only the children into care which in most cases means that they will leave school with no academic qualifications and are most likely to become homeless or drift into prostitution or crime.

For most of the 60,000 children in care in Britain the future outlook is bleak. Official figures show that 98% of these children come from broken homes or from a dysfunctional family, which probably means that they had never known the love and security of a loving family.

But it is not only children in care who are starved of love; there are millions of other children who are not taken into care but are nevertheless growing up in home environments where they feel unloved and insecure. Even in affluent families where children have all the material things they could wish to possess they may nevertheless not have the one thing that is most needed - the unquestionable knowledge of being loved.

Re-Examining Lifestyles

It is arguable that the greatest social need today is for a full-scale re-examination of personal lifestyles and values. What are the things that really matter to us? What is more valuable than anything else? If we lost all the material things that give us pleasure and provide us with comfort, what things do people hold as essential and that make life worth living? Surely the answer has to lie in our personal love relationships.

It may be that the worldwide economic recession and financial crisis that began in 2008 with the collapse of some of the world's most prestigious banks and powerful financial institutions will trigger just such a re-examination. The knock-on effect of the credit crunch introduced by the banks to deal with their own problems reached many sectors of the economy with great manufacturing industries such as General Motors and the Ford Motor Company and allied industrial plants all being affected, which shook the nations and impacted the lives of millions.

The speed with which this economic collapse spread took many people by surprise but those who have been watching world events over the past half-century and reading the Bible alongside their newspapers would *actually have been expecting* what has happened. The Bible speaks of a time coming when God will shake not only the nations but also the whole of creation. It is undeniable that there is a global shaking taking place in our lifetime - social, economic and physical. Geologists tell us that there have been more earthquakes and tsunamis in the past 50 years than at any time since records began.

The Icelandic volcano eruption in April 2010 that spread of cloud of dust and ash over most of Europe and closed off air traffic was a spectacular demonstration of the powerlessness of human beings when the forces of nature are unleashed. Many Christians saw the ash as symbolising a call for repentance, and that the grounding of air traffic leaving 7 million frustrated travellers and blocking the movement of freight, was a warning sign from God. It served to intensify the great financial crisis which has especially shaken the Western nations driving up unemployment and affecting most countries in the world.

Shaking the Nations

There are numerous biblical passages that speak of God shaking the nations such as Isaiah 2 from verse 12, *"The Lord Almighty has a day in store for all the proud and lofty, for all that is exalted and they will be humbled when he rises to shake the earth."* But the key Scripture is in Haggai 2.6-7,

"This is what the Lord Almighty says: 'In a little while I will once more shake the heavens and the earth and the dry land. I will shake all nations and the desired of all nations will come and I will fill this house with glory says the Lord Almighty'.

I've referred to this Scripture many times in the past twenty years and its link with Hebrews where it is repeated in 12.26 making it still in the future at the end of the first century AD. The significance of this prophecy in Hebrews is that it links the shaking of the nations with the coming of the Kingdom of God. That does not mean that it is speaking of the final consummation of the Kingdom at the end of the world; but it is speaking of a time coming when God will shake all the institutions of our human civilisation upon which people build their trust. The prophecy is referring to a time when "created things", the foundations of our materialistic world, will crumble dramatically; a time when people will be forced to review their lifestyles as well as their personal values and the corporate values of society.

What began happening in 2008 was not merely a shaking of the economy but of the whole social and economic foundations of Western society. The shaking of the banks triggered the exposure of corruption in one great institution after another, not only financial institutions but also social and political. In London, even the 'Mother of Parliaments' was shaken, causing worldwide astonishment, as Members of Parliament were exposed for dodgy dealings in handling their expenses and allowances. Just as the deeds of the bankers had been exposed showing greed and corruption, so too were politicians. The prophecy in Hebrews was becoming frighteningly fulfilled.

"Once more I will shake not only the earth but also the heavens. The words 'once more' indicate the removing of what can be shaken - that is, created things - so that what cannot be shaken may remain."
                                                                    Hebrews 12.26 - 27

A Paradigm Shift

The prophecy refers to earlier occasions when God had shaken the Earth. It then looks forward to another great shaking which will coincide with a paradigm shift in the spiritual realms that will be linked with a major step towards the establishment of the Kingdom of God on earth. This great shaking of the institutions of mammon in which most people put their trust will bring considerable hardship and suffering but it will also cause people to re-examine their personal values and lifestyles. This is why I'm excited to see these times because these are the days for which I have been waiting for some thirty years.

In the book *Towards the Dawn* published in 1980[1], I outlined the five major social institutions in Western society - Family, Education, the Economy, Law and Government, and Religion. I said that when any one of these five major social institutions experiences major change it affects all the others. At that time I saw that 4 out of the 5 were each generating major changes. The one relatively stable institution was the 'economy' which despite the ups and downs of boom and bust had remained relatively stable since the Great Depression of the 1920s. The changes in the family, education and law were so rapid and radical that unless there was a major change in the whole socio/political and economic direction in the nation we were heading for an indescribable disaster. That situation would shake the whole foundations of society throughout the Western nations and would be triggered by a collapse in the economy.

This is the point that was reached in 2008 and this is why it is essential that Christians, and especially Christian leaders, should understand the Biblical context of the socio/economic situation. Western nations had not experienced anything like this since the 1920s. European nations had not known times of hardship since the Second World War. Two generations had grown up in times of plenty with no experience of privation. Suddenly millions lost the security of employment and a regular income resulting in many re-examining their personal lifestyles and values. Young People were the most affected especially in Europe.

Re-Examining Social Values

For any such re-examination to be successful there has to be a yardstick against which to measure values. It is here that Western nations with their long history of Christianity should have been able to provide such a yardstick, but even a basic knowledge of the Bible is almost non-existent among younger people below the age of 40, especially in Britain and Europe where church decline has been sharp since the 1960s. Ignorance of the Bible has been accelerated in Britain and America because it is no longer taught in state schools. The concomitant rise of secular humanism has

---

[1] Clifford Hill, **Towards the Dawn**, Fount Books, Collins, London, Third Impression, 1982

had the effect of largely removing the "God dimension" from public life. People do not talk about God and over the past 50 years there has been a massive decline in respect for religion and especially for religious institutions such as the church. This has had a great effect upon family and marriage which are the building blocks of society, and provide identity and security to individuals as well as providing the means through which the culture, including social and personal values, is passed on to the next generation.

If there is to be a re-ordering of the values of society the starting point has to be in personal relationships, at the heart of which are our love relationships. For Christians, love and marriage are rooted in the teaching of the Bible and the revelation of God's love for us. Christians see our love for one another as a reflection of God's love for us which we know to be quite unmerited. The New Testament says that, *'while we were still sinners Christ died for us'* Romans 5.8, from which we gain an understanding that God loves us so much that he would go to any lengths to save us from the consequences of our own folly. God's greatest desire is that people would come to know his love for them which can transform their attitudes to others and all their personal relationships.

A Dramatic Incident

One of the most dramatic incidents in my own life brought this home to me.[2] It was one of the few times when I had actually heard God speak to me. My wife Monica and I were walking through the little Alpine village of Adelboden nestling high up in the Swiss Alps. It was the middle of January and we were heading to the place where the men's downhill of the World Cup was to be held. This was strange as we would both rank high in the ratings for the world's worst skiers. But we were not there for the skiing. We were joint speakers at a conference of European leaders of Campus Crusade. I had been speaking in the morning and we were both due to speak at the evening session, but we were free in the afternoon. So we set out to walk to the other side of the mountain where the downhill was to be run.

On the way there I had a growing awareness of the presence of God: it was not just a spiritual response to the beauty and grandeur of the scenery. I have learned to distinguish the times when God

---

[2] First published in Clifford Hill, **Tell My People I Love Them**, Fount Books, Collins, London, Third Impression,1985, pages 9 - 16.

draws particularly close to communicate a special message and I've learned at those times to be especially attentive and watchful. So it was with a heightened sense of perception and expectancy that we arrived at the foot of the slope and joined the huge crowd that had gathered to watch some of the world's most daring and skilful young men risking life and limb to hurl themselves down the mountainside, trying to reduce record-breaking times by mere fractions of a second. It was a thrilling sight and we entered fully into the spirit of the occasion, cheering the Swiss boys who were popular with the local crowd (there being no British competitors!)

Monica and I have always enjoyed most forms of sport, both as participants and as spectators, but this afternoon was different. I had a strangely compelling feeling that there was some other reason why we had come out there. It wasn't just to see the men's downhill ski event. I was sure that God had something to say to me and I eagerly watched every movement of the competitors and I even scanned the crowd around me for anything of significance through which God might speak to me.

Eventually it was all over. The last competitor completed his run; the presentations were made; the TV camera crews closed down their equipment and the crowd began to disperse. Several thousand people began to walk back into the town. As we joined the crowd I had a sense of disappointment and found myself saying, "Lord, have I missed something? Did I not have my eyes open to what you wanted to show me? Forgive me, Lord, if I have not been attentive."

The footpath back into Adelboden was narrow and winding, following the contours around the side of the mountain. It was slow going with the large crowd threading its way along the snow packed icy track which in some places was only four or five feet wide. At one point the pathway turned a sharp bend hugging the mountain face on one side, and on the other side there was a low wooden guard-rail protecting a steep snow-covered slope running down towards the edge of the ledge with a sheer drop onto rocks below.

A Near Tragedy

We had hardly turned the corner when the air was suddenly rent with a piercing scream of a child just behind me. She had evidently missed her footing coming round the bend on the outside of the crowd, slipped under the guard-rail and was now sliding helplessly down the steep slope towards the edge. I swung round, and together with hundreds of others, stood frozen to the spot powerlessly watching the small figure of a three or four-year-old child sliding down the mountainside on her stomach, feet first, with arms outstretched screaming with the full power of her lungs and her eyes looking imploringly upwards. I doubt whether I will ever forget the look of helpless terror in that child's eyes as her body gathered speed on its way down towards almost certain death.

Before I could even take in the full horror of the situation another dramatic event occurred that was to leave an indelible picture in my mind. Within seconds, as the first screams from the child were echoing from mountains across the valley, a man hurled himself through the crowd, leapt the guard-rail and ran down the slope with such incredible speed that he rapidly began to overtake the child still screaming at the top of her voice. It was little short of a miracle that he managed to keep his balance on the acute slope - actually running down the mountainside! A few more strides and he reached the child, sweeping her up into his arms, and then was lost from sight for a few moments in a flurry of snow as he stopped himself just yards short of the edge of the slope. He stood there for what seemed a long time with the child's arms flung round his neck clinging tightly and sobbing loudly.

An Amazing Rescue

The man, later identified as the child's father, steadied himself in preparation for the dangerous climb back up the snow-covered slope. The climb seemed to take ages as he dug into the deep snow, testing each foothold before taking a step, ensuring that it was safe to take him with the additional weight of the child in his arms. Eventually he reached the guard-rail where there were plenty of willing hands stretched out to help him onto the pathway and to lift the little girl over the rail into the comfort of her mother's arms.

As I watched the father standing there so close to the sheer drop onto the rocks below and as I watched him on his slow ascent to safety it is then that I believe God spoke to me.

"This is what I brought you here to see. You saw how that child was sliding towards certain death. You saw how her eyes were looking up to her father and you heard how she cried for help. You saw how her father responded immediately, not hesitating to assess the danger to himself, but flung himself down the mountainside to rescue his child. That is how I love my children."

A Message of Love

"Lord," I responded, "That is wonderful! Your love is just amazing!"

Immediately, I felt a sense of rebuke as though God was saying.

"Why do you say that? Do you think that my love is less than that of a human father? Did I not create him? Did I not make him capable of such a love for his child? Am I less than my own creation? I am God. There is no other! I created the universe and I created human beings in my own image. My love is at least as great as human love and a million times more and a million times more."

It was then that I heard the words that were to have a long-term impact on my ministry. Very clearly the words came to me,

"Tell my people I love them. Tell my people I love them."

From somewhere in the back of my mind there came the words of a song:

Tell my people I love them,
Tell my people I care.
When they feel far away from me,
Tell my people I'm there.

We walked along the path back into the town, silently re-living the drama of the last few minutes, each of us conscious of the presence of the Living God, 'lost in wonder, love and praise'.

In that little drama of human love we had both witnessed a tiny glimpse of God's great saving purposes for his children. The fresh mountain air, the winding path, the breathtaking view across the valley, all seemed to take on a new significance of the God of Creation revealing his everlasting love for the people whom he had created in his image. I think we both felt a little bit like Moses standing on another mountain when he took off his shoes feeling that the very ground on which he stood was holy with the presence of Almighty God.

The experience on the mountainside transformed the evening message especially as we sang:

Mine is an unchanging love
Higher than the heights above
Deeper than the depths beneath

Re-Living the Drama

There have been many times during a sleepless night when I have re-lived that drama on the mountainside and asked myself the question, 'If that had been my child would I have jumped the guard-rail and run down to save her?' I would like to think that the answer is, 'Yes I would!' But I have never been in that position so I can't be absolutely certain. The one certain thing I do know is that I made no attempt to go and save someone else's child. I don't find that a very comfortable thought. But, of course, there were scores of other men near enough to try to save the child, but only one man actually risked his life and ran down the mountainside to save the child - her father!

This powerful illustration of a father's love has given me so much more understanding of the love of God our Father; the Father of our Lord Jesus Christ. It was Jesus who taught us to know His Father and to call him *'Abba'*, 'Daddy', just as that little girl embraced her daddy when he saved her life.

The greatest tragedy in the contemporary world is the way in which family life has collapsed in Western nations leaving so many children bereft of love and security. In many inner-city areas broken families have led to children and young people forming gangs that are often blamed for the high crime rate today.

The gang forms an important part of social structure and culture in inner-city areas where it is a substitute for the family, providing identity, belongingness, security and behavioural regulations. But the one thing the gang cannot provide is love - true, genuine, undemanding and unselfish love. Yet this is what all human beings desire more than anything else.

That kind of love comes from God: nowhere else: ***only from God.***

GOD'S LOVE FOR THE UNLOVED

This chapter deals with the message God sent to his people in exile in Babylon in response to their cries for help as they felt unloved and unwanted. The message shows God's tender loving care for those who are oppressed and who have nothing to offer in return for his love.

Trafalgar Square in the heart of London was packed with a large crowd on a warm summer day. They were mainly Christians who had responded to a call to come together on Pentecost Sunday to celebrate the birthday of the church and the coming of the Holy Spirit. Inevitably there were also members of the general public mixed in with the crowd. It was a joyful occasion with lots of singing as well as short addresses and readings recalling the events recorded in Acts chapter 2 when the disciples were in 'the upper room' where they had a remarkable experience of the Holy Spirit and they spilled out onto the crowded streets of Jerusalem declaring the amazing message that Jesus who had been crucified outside the city was actually alive - resurrected by the power of God!

At one point in the Trafalgar Square gathering, the leader said that we were now going to share 'the peace' with one another. He explained that in many churches Christians greet each other by shaking hands or even giving a hug and saying "Peace be with you". He said that on this special occasion he wanted us all to remind each other about Jesus' teaching that *"God so loved the world that he sent his Son"* John 3.16. "We're going to share God's love with each other" he said. We were to do this by saying to the person next to us, "Jesus loves you!"

A Brief Encounter

I was quite enthusiastic about this because standing next to me on my left was a rather nice looking young woman. I was not against giving her a hug and telling her that Jesus loved her. But then the leader said I want you to turn to the person on your right.

Next to me on my right was a shabbily dressed man who had evidently been sleeping rough and who clearly had not had a bath for some time. I had already become aware of him through senses other than sight! And I had been steadily averting my gaze and trying to draw my breath when looking the other way.

Suddenly I was challenged. Did I really believe that God loved all the world? Did I have sufficient of the love of God to be able to share it with this man? Then, in the act of turning to him, looking him in the eye for the first time, I felt a wave of compassion and it was easy to put my arms around him and tell him that Jesus loved him. The outcome was remarkable; tears filled his eyes and his whole body was deeply shaken with emotion. I lost sight of him in the crowd after the event but I've no doubt that at that moment something unique happened in his life as he became conscious of the love of God surrounding him and speaking into his inmost being.

We all get these brief encounters when we have just a moment to communicate a life-changing message to one of God's children who has a unique need at that moment. All we have to do is to be obedient to the prompting of the Holy Spirit - in the words of Mary, the mother of Jesus, at the wedding in Cana of Galilee, *"Do whatever he tells you!"*[1] If we do whatever he tells us we can leave the rest to him.

An Outrageous Message

"The Lord comforts his people and will have compassion on his afflicted ones."
                                                                Isaiah 49.13

This was essentially the message of the prophets of Israel who learned to listen to the Lord and to be obedient to him. In Isaiah 49 there is an earth-shattering message: that the people of Israel were to be *"a light for the Gentiles"*[2] so that they could bring God's salvation to the ends of the earth. It was just too bizarre to have been thought up by human reasoning!

The message was so outrageous that it could only have come as a direct revelation from God. Just look at the circumstances. The city of Jerusalem was in ruins; the flower of the nation's young men had been slaughtered; the survivors had been taken into slavery in Babylon. Now, more than a generation later, God

---

[1] See John 2.5
[2] See Isaiah 49.6

sends them a prophecy that they are to be his emissaries to the world; that their special mission is to teach all the Gentile nations about God's way of salvation.

It's not hard to imagine how the oppressed people in Babylon would have received this prophecy, no doubt with a mixture of scorn and disbelief. They were a small company of expatriates trying to maintain their faith in the face of the contempt of their conquerors who continually reminded them that the God of Israel had been defeated by the gods of Babylon. Day after day they were humiliated, even being commanded by their captors to entertain them with sacred songs of Zion. They wrote a song expressing their despair,

"By the Rivers of Babylon we sat and wept when we remembered Zion. There on the poplars we hung our harps, for there our captors asked us for songs, our tormentors demanded songs of joy; they said, 'Sing us one of the songs of Zion!' How can we sing the songs of the Lord while in a foreign land?"   Psalm 137.1 - 4

But it was to this distressed and despairing group of slaves that God sent this historic message that he was about to overthrow the mighty Babylonian Empire, to release the captives, to send them back to their ancient capital of Jerusalem from where he would send out a message to all nations on earth. The message would be fully revealed through his Messiah whom he would send to them.

Overcoming Despair

Of course, they found it difficult to accept this prophecy and Isaiah[3] had to work hard to build up their faith and confidence in God so that they could be ready to undertake the arduous 1,000 mile journey back to Jerusalem by foot once they were released. His biggest challenge was to overcome their despair and hopelessness and to restore their faith in God. They believed that they were an abandoned people; that their God was powerless to help. Isaiah had to convince them that the God of Abraham, Isaac and Jacob was in fact the Creator of the whole Universe; that he held the destiny of nations in his hands "as a drop in a bucket" [4]

---

[3] See extended footnote on the Prophet Isaiah at the end of this chapter, page 36

[4] See Isaiah 40.15

as he put it; that the God of Israel was the all-powerful Sovereign who could raise up and put down rulers of the nations.

Moreover, God was a covenant-keeping God who actually loved his people. He had made a promise to his people hundreds of years earlier that he would never forget. The prophet set about convincing people that it was actually impossible for God to forget his people; *"Can a mother forget the baby at her breast?"* he asked[5]. Certainly all the women would have understood exactly what he was saying, for if they were breastfeeding a baby, even if the infant did not cry, after a number of hours her breasts would fill and the discomfort or pain would certainly remind her of the baby.

The Prophet continued with the analogy saying that it was even more impossible for God to forget his people than for a mother to forget her baby. The young mother might be momentarily distracted by many other demands upon her time but with God there is never a moment when his people are out of his care and attention. *"See!" God says, "I have engraved your name on the palms of my hands."* [6]

All the people would have known the meaning of this. A mother interceding for her son, or a husband for his wife, would often write the name upon the palms of their hands and lift them in intercession as though they were bringing the loved one, for whom they were pleading, into the presence of God. In this analogy Isaiah says that God has not merely written the name of his beloved people on his hands but has actually engraved the name of their city upon his hands. Although her walls were in ruins they were always before him and they symbolised the people with whom he had made a solemn covenant. He could never forget them and he loved them so much that the day would come when he would overthrow their conquerors and take them back to the land he had given to their fathers.

This message of God's tender love and care for those who were desperate, who felt deserted and in despair, expresses the very heart of the message God wants his people to take to the world. It needs to be heard by all those who feel betrayed by other human beings such as those who are the innocent victims of

---

[5] See Isaiah 49.15

[6] See Isaiah 49.16

family breakdown. Across the Western world there are millions of young women who have been deserted by husbands or partners, leaving them to struggle to bring up children on their own. They need to hear the message that God loves them even more than the most faithful husband and he will never leave them alone.

There are also millions of children who have witnessed the violent quarrels of their parents and sometimes feel that they are to blame. They feel worthless and sometimes try to think of ways of punishing themselves. Some children resort to self-harm because they have been told that they are worthless. So many young lives today are ruined by thoughtless adults or other young people who tell them that they are rubbish. Other children see themselves as ugly and even try to take their own lives.

Love Transforms

A teenage girl appeared on the BBC programme, 'Songs of Praise' in September 2009 saying how she had seen herself as fat and ugly and was unable to look at herself in the mirror. Then she found Jesus and was amazed to discover how much he loved her. This changed her whole outlook upon life. She had thought about Jesus' teaching that we should not only love God but also love our neighbour *as ourselves!* It was from this that she learned to love herself as Jesus loved her. She had recently bought a full-length mirror which she saw as a measure of the change that the love of God had brought into her life. She no longer despised herself but saw herself as Jesus sees her.

It is this transforming love of God that is so greatly needed in the Western nations today where the fragmentation of family life has had a devastating impact upon millions of people. Even in those families that have not been split apart by divorce or separation it is not uncommon for individuals to feel lonely and unsupported, especially teenagers going through the emotional stress of puberty. In many homes members of the family never eat a meal together and don't even possess a dining room table. Food is just taken at different times with a plate in front of the television or up in the bedroom in front of a computer playing computer games or getting onto Facebook. Family life is non-existent. Life across the Internet has become the post-modern reality for many! The impact upon relationships is devastating; not only on family life but also in social relationships.

Relationship Poverty

Our human nature is created to have relationships with each other - not to live in isolation or to live in the unreal environment of cyber-reality tapping out messages to people we've never met and with whom we have no face-to-face contact. Even our language of communication becomes distorted. This happens not just in the teenage years. It's happening in infancy where young mothers have no time to give to their infants. They sit them in front of the television or leave them at a nursery or playgroup where their language skills are not developed and they simply squeal to one another or take what they demand without learning social skills. Teachers in reception classes in primary schools say that many children come to them with limited vocabulary because mothers have never spent time bonding with their babies and talking to them to help them to develop verbal communication skills. Without such skills our ability to form relationships is severely impaired.

It is in this respect that Christians need to understand and be able to respond to this 'relationship poverty' that is a growing characteristic of a degenerating civilisation. God is a relational being who has created human beings to be in a personal relationship with him and with each other. That is our natural environment and we only become fully developed as human beings when we are in a right relationship with God and with each other. Being in right relationships is an essential part of the teaching of the Bible from Genesis to Revelation. Isaiah reports God saying,

"I am the Lord your God, who teaches you what is best for you, who directs you in the way you should go. If only you had paid attention to my commandments, your peace would have been like a river, your righteousness like the waves of the sea".

Isaiah 48.17 - 18

Right Relationships

The reference to 'righteousness' means right relationships both with God and with our fellow human beings. In fact, the teaching of Scripture is that we can never be fully in right relationships with others unless we get our relationship right with God. This is why Jesus says that we should seek first the Kingdom of God and his righteousness and everything else falls into place. Jesus told parables about the Kingdom of God being like someone who discovers a priceless pearl and sacrifices everything else in order to possess it. Once you discover this personal relationship with God nothing else compares with it - you find an almost indescribable peace that takes you into a new dimension.

You suddenly discover that God is with you all the time and you find yourself talking to him when you're alone, or when you are driving, or even when you've got lots of people around you. When you're travelling on a train or bus you can be having a silent conversation with the Lord. This, of course, is prayer! The whole of your prayer life changes when you discover this personal relationship with God. Prayer changes from the recital of set words to an intimate conversation. This is how the prophets of Israel communicated with God. They didn't have the benefit of knowing Jesus as we do. We know that Jesus is constantly at the Father's side interceding for us; as Paul says, *"the Spirit intercedes for the saints"*.   Romans 8.27

The Council of the Lord

The prophets had to discover God before the coming of Messiah. They didn't know the teaching of Jesus on the Fatherhood of God. But they learned to get into the presence of God, sometimes by going away and climbing a mountain or going out into a desert place to be alone. Jeremiah called this experience, "getting into the Council of the Lord". He didn't just talk to God. He discovered that when you have a personal relationship with God communication becomes a two-way experience. He learned to be quiet and to listen as well as to pour out his heart before the Lord.

This was the way all the writing prophets of Israel carried out their ministries. They would observe what was happening in their local community, in the nation, and events on the international scene. Then they would "spread it before the Lord" - telling God all the things that they had seen and then quietly awaiting God's response. The prophet Amos is a good example of this method. He was a Southerner who was sent up to the North of Israel to take the word of God, but, as a new arrival, he wisely did not just stand up in the northern capital of Samaria and begin public proclamation. He carefully went about doing his research. He watched the practices of the merchants in the marketplace and he listened to the conversations of the housewives, the tales of the travellers, and then he took all this into his prayer times. When he was sure of the response he was hearing, he was able to declare, *"This is what the Lord is saying..."* People listened, even when they didn't like what they were hearing, because the words of the prophet carried a divine authority. People recognised that here was a man who had been in the presence of God.

When you discover the secret of a personal relationship with God it changes your entire outlook upon life and, of course, most importantly, it changes your relationships with others. And this is the message that God wants us to take to others in our family, in our local community and into our places of work. God has chosen this way of working - through those who have responded to his love and come into a personal relationship with him. It is a relationship that is so attractive that we cannot help sharing it with others. In fact, we cannot keep it to ourselves! Other people can see that there is something special in the way we treat them and there is something attractive about our lifestyle that creates bridges of communication. If all God's people were living attractive lives the transforming power of the love of God would be reaching out through our everyday contacts and we would not need special meetings or campaigns to tell people the message of the gospel.

Sacrificial Love

As the Research Director for the Family Matters Institute I was doing research for a report on the role of grandparents in family life today. I received many case studies of grandparents taking responsibilities for children following parental marriage or relationship breakdown[7]. Many of them were making considerable personal sacrifices in order to care for the children. There was one outstanding example of love that reflected the self-sacrificial love of God that goes on giving without counting the cost. They were an elderly couple who described their circumstances in quiet, non-emotional terms that spoke volumes for the endless hours of patient love devoted to a child. Their story is best told in their own words.

"We are parents to an eight year old boy who is actually our great-grandchild but we have raised him since he was a baby. He is the eldest of our five great-grandchildren. Both his parents became drug addicts and unable to care for him. We took him into our home when he was six months old. That was eight years ago.

---

[7] Hill, Brooks, Cook, Clark; **Do Grandparents Matter?** The Impact of Grandparenting on the Well-Being of Children; Family Matters Institute; 2009

"Our grandson left home when his child was only four months old and he has not seen the boy since that day. His wife (our granddaughter-in-law) was sent to prison when her child was six months old so we took responsibility for the baby. She is back in prison now serving a second sentence. She also has not come to see their child since he was a baby so he does not know either of his natural parents. As far as he is concerned we are his parents.

"We love our great-grandson very dearly although we know that we are not able to do for him all the things that young parents would do. We are not physically able to join in sports activities and financially we cannot provide him with all the things a growing child needs.

"Except for Child Benefit and Child Tax Credit Allowance we get no financial help. We pay for everything with our senior citizens' pensions and my husband's Army pension. We do not qualify for anything else. We even have to pay for school milk and school dinners. We gladly share with him what we have although we know that he is deprived of many of the things other children have and this grieves us."

I have only printed here a small part of their report but it is sufficient to show the love and care this couple devote to a child. Obviously they worry about what will happen to the boy when they become too old and frail to care for him adequately, but their trust is in the Lord from whom they draw strength day by day and they leave the future in his hands.

God has promised that when we put our trust in him he will never leave us alone: he has promised us the abiding presence of the Holy Spirit. Jesus said, *"If you love me, you will obey what I command. And I will ask the Father, and he will give you another Counsellor to be with you for ever - the Spirit of truth... you know him, for he lives with you and will be in you. I will not leave you as orphans; I will come to you."* John 14.15 - 17

The 'command' Jesus was referring to was to love other people. When we obey that command we put ourselves in the very centre of his will and we see him fulfil his promise to be with us forever and in all circumstances.

Practical Love

Putting our trust in God is an exciting thing to do especially when we find ourselves out of our comfort zone and doing things that we never imagined we would ever do, as in the case of the elderly couple caring for a great-grandchild. Their story is not unique: there are literally thousands of grandparents who are undertaking the responsibilities of parenting young children because of family breakdown. There are others who are acting as surrogate grandparents through churches that have outreach programmes to meet the increasing need for practical help in the community as family life continues to break down and single mothers struggle to bring up their children alone.

It is encouraging to see that among the many great things happening today Christians are not sitting in church waiting for people to come to them but are going out actively showing the love of God in practical situations. There is a wide variety of different kinds of social outreach. One of the most effective is the growing movement of 'Street Pastors'[8] - people of all ages, many of them young people, who are going on to the streets in city centres or market towns in the evenings and weekends. They are particularly there to help young people who have been drinking too much and who find themselves in dangerous situations. Many lives have been changed through simple acts of kindness that have led to conversations about faith and the sharing of the gospel, or opened the way for prayer.

There are reports from all over the country of life-changing encounters where Christians are taking the love of God out to the people in ordinary situations. It would appear that more people are making decisions for Christ on the streets of our towns and cities than in churches! This, of course, is how it was in the beginning, in the early days of the New Testament Church - when 'church' meant a 'community of believers' and not a building!

All the emphasis in those days was upon relationships: the relationship between the believer and Jesus and relationships between each other. It was these relationships that were so attractive to others. Luke has painted a little abbreviated picture of the life of the Christian community in the days shortly after

---

[8] *www.streetpastors.org.uk*

Pentecost. *"They broke bread in their homes and ate together with glad and sincere hearts, praising God and enjoying the favour of all the people. And the Lord added to their number daily those who were being saved".*   Acts 2.46 - 47

A Fresh Move of God

It may be that what we are seeing is just the beginning of a fresh move of God to communicate his love to those who have never known the meaning of true love; to those who have been crushed and disappointed by their experience of life and especially those who feel worthless and rejected by others. These are the people who are especially loved by Jesus who was himself despised and rejected and experienced the worst kind of cruelty and suffering that could be inflicted upon a human being by other humans. He understands those who feel unloved and cannot believe that anyone could love them. To them he says, *"I love you and you are precious in my sight."*

These words come in Isaiah 43 at the climax of a most amazing promise of the love of God to his people. It is expressed as a personal message to each individual and is intended to convey the intimacy between God and his chosen ones. It is not just the nation as a mass of humanity whom God is addressing but each individual who is precious in the sight of the Lord. *"Fear not"* he says. *"For I have **redeemed** you"* which expresses a one-to-one relationship. That phrase was quite ancient, going back hundreds of years in the Hebrew Family Law. It referred to the act of a relative stepping in to pay off the debt of a relative who had fallen into debt and had been imprisoned or enslaved. We see evidence of this same phrase being used in the account of Ruth and her kinsman, Boaz, who rescued her from poverty and married her.[9]

Setting the People Free

If we are really to understand the impact of this message upon the people of Judah enslaved in Babylon, we have to empty our minds of our highly spiritualised use of the term "redemption" in modern Christian theology. It had a simple practical meaning in ancient Israel and was regularly used in certain family situations. But for the exiles it meant that God had not forgotten or forsaken

---

[9] See Ruth chapter 4

them. They were still his people in a covenant relationship with their God, even though they were in the most desperate and humiliating situation. They were still part of God's family and as Kinsman Redeemer he was acting to buy them back from Babylon.

The truly remarkable thing in this passage is that the verbs are expressed in the "perfect" tense, meaning an action that had already been accomplished. *"I **have** redeemed you; I **have** summoned you by name."* Yet the people were still in captivity in Babylon. To the prophet the vision he had seen of God's work in the political turmoil of the rise and fall of empires was so real that he could speak of it in the past tense, as though it had already happened!

"You are mine" is the comforting personal assurance addressed collectively to the nation, but expressed individually to include each one of his people. The journey back to Jerusalem would be rough and tough, but God would be with them. Water and fire were symbols of difficulties and dangers ahead but nothing would be too great a problem for them. They would not be burned or destroyed, for God was in control of the nations; the Holy One of Israel was their Saviour. He would ensure that as the warring empires of humanity battled for supremacy, his own people would be protected and would reach their homeland in safety.

You Are Mine!

It is a beautiful message of reassurance addressed to each believer; to all who put their trust in God. We are not just an inconsequential part of the great mass of humanity. We are each one precious in God's sight. He says to each of us, "You are mine! You belong to me in a personal relationship and I will never leave you alone!" When we face dangers or very difficult situations, God's assurance is a personal guarantee of his love, *"When you pass through the waters, I will be with you... When you walk through the fire you will not be burned"*. Isaiah 43.2

In the same passage we come to the statement, *"You are precious and honoured in my sight and I love you"* Isaiah 43.4. This must rank high among the most beautiful statements in the Bible expressing the love of God. The words are in the first person singular.

Isaiah is reporting what he has heard from the mouth of the Lord about his unconditional love for his people.

A Message of Love

The truly remarkable thing about this pronouncement is revealed when it is seen in light of the condition of the people. They were a bedraggled, powerless remnant of a once powerful and proud nation. Far from their homeland and plunged into slavery in a foreign land, oppressed by a cruel people whose language they did not understand; they were a defeated and dispirited alien minority in Babylon, the capital of the mightiest empire so far known to the world.

It was amazing that the people of Judah had even managed to maintain their national identity. But the most stunning news was this pronouncement by the prophet. It is a staggering pronouncement when you think of whom he is addressing. Here was the Lord who had created the whole universe, who set the stars in their orbits and held the nations in his hands, the Lord of all creation speaking to this tiny despised community and saying, *"You are precious and honoured in my sight, and I love you."* It was a truly breathtaking declaration.

As if to underline the incredible difference between the God of history and the little group of displaced aliens the pronouncement was followed by a promise, *"Because I love you I will give men in exchange for you and people in exchange for your life"* Isaiah 43.4. The clear meaning of this is that God was in control of all nations during one of the most turbulent periods of political change in the history of the ancient world and there was much more to come.

Through the international upheavals that were about to take place God would ensure that his own beloved people were released from Babylon and returned to the land of their fathers. They would come from all corners of the Babylonian Empire and this great re-gathering of those called by the name of the Lord would bring glory to God. This was his purpose in calling Israel to be his chosen people; to be a light to the nations and to reveal his love and purposes to the whole world.

To all those who feel worthless, despised and rejected by the world, this message of God's love is addressed today, through the Lord Jesus our Messiah. We all get discouraged and depressed at times. There are periods in life when nothing seems to go right and everything is hard. In such times we get tired and dispirited. That was the condition of the exiles in Babylon to whom God sent this message. He is sending the same message today to all those who are finding life hard. In our lowest moments, even though we may have sinned, as Israel had, the word of God is addressed to us. *"You are precious and honoured in my sight and I love you... Do not be afraid, for I am with you"*.   Isaiah 43.4 - 5

This beautifully expresses the love of God towards the lowly of heart.

---

footnote from page 25

[3] All biblical scholars recognise that there is a difference in style, language and message in sections of the Book of Isaiah. Chapters 1 - 35 are generally thought to be the work of the Eighth Century prophet known as 'Isaiah of Jerusalem'. Chapters 36 - 39 are historical and are largely drawn from the account in 2 Kings and 2 Chronicles. Chapters 40 - 55 all refer to the closing years of the Babylonian exile while Chapters 56 - 66 are relevant to the early post-exilic period following the overthrow of Babylon by Cyrus the Persian in 539 BC. These chapters are best understood when seen against the background of the hardships endured by the first wave of exiles who returned to Judah and began the resettlement of the land and the rebuilding of Jerusalem.

Some scholars believe that the whole Book of Isaiah was written by one man in the Eighth Century to whom God revealed messages that would be relevant hundreds of years later in the Sixth and Fifth Centuries. Others believe that the Isaianic School of Prophecy begun by Isaiah of Jerusalem continued for many years and that God raised up men in each generation to fulfil his purposes and to bring his word to the people among whom he lived and shared their experiences.

It is outside the purposes of this book to enter into detailed textual criticism so when reference is made to a text that is clearly Eighth Century the prophet is referred to as 'Isaiah of Jerusalem'. In all other textual references the prophet is simply addressed as 'Isaiah'.

Chapter Two

GOD'S LOVE IN FAMILY AND MARRIAGE

The Prophet Hosea had a turbulent marriage but his unbreakable love for his unfaithful wife won her love in the end. From this Hosea learned a unique message about the unbreakable love of God.

Family Breakdown

Despite the fact that there is such a high rate of marriage breakdown in 21st century Britain marriage remains extremely popular. Nine out of ten schoolgirls aged 13 to 15 say that they hope to get married one day.[1] This is despite the fact that many of them will already have experienced the breakdown of their parents' marriage or relationship. Children have strong ideals and to live in a happy stable relationship and 'be happy ever after' has a strong appeal.

The breakdown of family life has become a major social feature in all Western nations and in Britain many families have become increasingly recognised as dysfunctional and the state has to intervene to protect children. Over the past two or three decades there have been numerous research reports about family life in America and Europe all of which have shown that marriage provides the most stable and satisfying relationship for adults and the best environment for bringing up children. There is a great deal written in the Bible about love and marriage, and about relationships between the genders and between generations. But there is one book that features problems in marriage from which much can be learnt. It is the Book of Hosea.

Hosea's love life was a rollercoaster. In the Book bearing his name he gives a frank and honest firsthand account. It is a story that has everything you would find in a modern novel – unrequited love, adultery, broken relationships, reconciliation, and the final triumph of true love. The uniqueness of this account is that it is not only a true story but it is used by the prophet to show the amazing

---

[1] See Clifford Hill, **'Sex Under Sixteen'**, Family Education Trust, London 2000 page 30

love of God for his people that transcends their sinfulness and their unfaithfulness.

The love of God for Israel is taken for granted by most of the prophets. It is for this reason that God's love, which is the central theme of the New Testament, is not dealt with at length by most of the Hebrew prophets. Their major concern is with Israel's **response** to the love of God and with the consequences of failing to respond rightly. This is why the Prophet Hosea's account of his traumatic marriage is so valuable in understanding the love of God in the context of our human sins and unfaithfulness.

An Unusual Marriage

In the first three chapters of Hosea the prophet describes his marriage to Gomer. This is one of the rare occasions in scripture in which God actually calls for one of his servants to be 'unequally yoked'; married to a young woman who did not share his faith. There was, of course, a special purpose for this.

Hosea was the first of the great eighth century prophets of Israel to speak explicitly of the love of God. In fact, he was probably the first to perceive the depths of God's love. Hosea's own turbulent marriage and his unbreakable love for his unfaithful wife were the background to the revelation the prophet received of God's unbreakable love for Israel. But it is a mistake to think that it was the unfortunate experience of Hosea's own broken marriage that led him to an understanding of God's love. In fact, he was specifically instructed by God to marry a girl whom he knew to be involved in harlotry. This was to give the prophet a first-hand experience of the pain involved in such a relationship. Through this Hosea was to hear something of God's pain because of the spiritual harlotry of Israel in worshipping other gods.

Naming the Children

When God began to speak through Hosea, the Lord said to him, *"'Go, take to yourself an adulterous wife and children of unfaithfulness, because the land is guilty of the vilest adultery in departing from the Lord." So he married Gomer daughter of Diblaim, and she conceived and bore him a son. Then the Lord said to Hosea, "Call him Jezreel"* (which means 'Disaster')'.

Hosea gave each of his children a name that expressed what God was saying to the nation.

'Gomer conceived again and gave birth to a daughter. Then the Lord said to Hosea, "Call her Lo-Ruhamah, ('Not Loved') *for I will no longer show love to the house of Israel."*

'After she had weaned Lo-Ruhamah, Gomer had another son. Then the Lord said, "Call him Lo Ammi, ('Not Mine) *for you are not my people, and I am not your God"'.*   Hosea 1. 2 - 9

Clearly there were problems in being the children of a prophet!

A Dramatic Parable

Some commentators hold that Gomer was a common street prostitute. There is good evidence not to accept this view and it is much more likely that she was one of the beautiful young maidens in the local Canaanite shrine. In taking her as his wife the prophet, as a man of God, no doubt caused a minor sensation in Israel. Everyone would have known her background and for a prophet of the God of Israel to take a wife who had been involved in temple prostitution, however beautiful she was, this was outrageous. The whole nation would have been talking about it. But this was just what God intended!

Hosea's marriage was to be seen as a dramatic parable symbolising God's marriage with Israel through his covenant relationship. Israel was an adulterous nation playing the harlot with other gods. For Hosea, his marriage was a prophetic action showing that God continued to love his covenant nation despite the fact that they were having intercourse with other gods. He chose to enter into a marriage covenant with a girl whose parents had sold her to the local temple harem where girls were used in acts of sexual symbolism by the cultic priests.

The Canaanite shrines were dedicated to Hadad, who was usually known simply as the local Baal. He was variously regarded as the lord, husband, or owner of the people in his area. The land, which came under the jurisdiction of the local Baal, was regarded as his wife, which he fertilised with rain. In order to ensure that the land produced a good crop, the local shrines engaged in sympathetic magic to induce Baal's intercourse with the earth through a variety of sexual rites. Local girls were often dedicated to the Baal and became part of a shrine harem available to the priests and male worshippers. There is good evidence that Gomer was one of these girls although it is not clear whether or not she had as yet been used in these practises, although we assume so.

Through his marriage to Gomer, who had been committed to ritual harlotry in an institution dedicated to an intimate relationship with Baal, Hosea dramatised the religious situation of Israel and the predicament of God, who had entered into a covenant relationship with a people who were playing the harlot with Baal.

Delayed Love

There is no evidence that Hosea loved Gomer when they first married. His beautiful, tender love for her grew later. In fact, the text suggests that his love came *after* her unfaithfulness rather than before. The first instruction he received from God was to *'go and take a wife'*. It was only after she had left him that Hosea was told to love her and to *'love her as the Lord loves the Israelites'*.

Hosea 3.1

In the first few years Hosea saw his marriage purely in terms of the conduct of his prophetic ministry. He used his wife for that purpose. Indeed, one cannot help having sympathy for Gomer. She was what today we would describe as the victim of ritual child abuse. She had been used by men the whole of her young adult life, first in the temple of Baal and now in her marriage.

Even though she was legally married, her husband used her for his own peculiar religious purposes. Her first child he named 'Disaster.' Her second child he called 'Not Loved.' Then her third child he called 'Not Mine.' Her embarrassment and shame at the naming ceremony was just too much to bear. In the presence of family, neighbours and friends, when she presented her baby to the priest and her husband was asked to name the child he said, 'This child is "Not mine" '.

That was the last straw! She left him and returned to the harem. It is entirely possible that Gomer simply did not understand the prophetic symbolism of what to her appeared to be Hosea's outrageous behaviour. But Gomer's return to the temple of Baal was seen by Hosea as yet another piece of vivid symbolism. Israel, although legitimately married to the Lord, ran away to the temple of Baal and worshipped idols.

Love and Patience

It was probably at this point, through his own experience, that Hosea began to perceive something unique in the love and patience of God for his people. He suddenly became aware of his own love for his wife. He genuinely missed Gomer and longed for her to return to him. Knowing the kind of things that were happening to her in that pagan temple sharpened his anxiety and deepened his compassion for her. Then God spoke to him again and told him to go and redeem his wife **and to love her**.

'The Lord said to me, "Go, show your love to your wife again, though she is loved by another and is an adulteress. Love her as the Lord loves the Israelites, though they turn to other gods and love the sacred raisin cakes." So I bought her for fifteen shekels of silver and about a homer and a lethek of barley.

'Then I told her, "You are to live with me for many days, you must not be a prostitute or be intimate with any man, and I will live with you." For the Israelites will live for many days without king or prince, without sacrifice or sacred stones, without ephod or idol. Afterwards the Israelites will return and seek the Lord their God and David their king. They will come trembling to the Lord and to his blessings in the last days'.   Hosea 3.1 - 5

In returning to her old way of life Gomer had now gone, not as a 'novice' or child-prostitute placed in the temple harem by her parents, but as a mature *married* woman deliberately choosing to enter a new, but *adulterous*, relationship. The effect was that she was now bound to the shrine in a way that could be broken only by purchase – by being 'redeemed', hence Hosea had to pay a 'ransom' or a 'redemption price.'

If she had simply been a common prostitute he would not have had to pay anything to take her back. The ransom was also a highly symbolic act by the prophet, who saw that Israel had forsaken the Lord and was committing spiritual adultery with idols. Only God could redeem his sinful people.

Symbols of Love

Once Gomer was back in his household Hosea protected her so that she could not sin again, and he added to the symbolism by refraining from sexual intercourse with her until she returned his love, therefore making the love union complete.

Hosea's dramatic actions symbolised the activity of the love of God in a number of highly significant ways. Through the prophet we see the love of God: first, in breaking the bonds of sin; secondly in setting the prisoner free; and thirdly in paying the redemption price to accomplish both of these. Through Hosea's marriage God was providing a poignant human parable of love and redemption that centuries later would be accomplished through his own beloved son on the cruel tree at Calvary.

The love of God was again symbolised in the way Hosea protected Gomer from further exploitation, and the beautiful way he waited for his beloved wife to return his love. He would not force her. He simply kept on loving her and waiting patiently for her. Eventually she responded to his love.

Through Hosea we see the love of God which overcomes false love to produce true love; which protects in order to set free; and which goes to any lengths to redeem.

Through it all, there is the pathos of the prophet who loves a wife, who is unfaithful to him; who loves her sufficiently to purchase her back from slavery to sin in order to restore her to himself; and who loves her so much that he will not impose his love upon her. Rather, he waits until she realises his great love for her and is able to respond and thus complete the conditions for a perfect love union.

A Love Union

In Hosea's marriage that started so disastrously but ended in a beautiful love union, we see dramatised the amazing, unbreakable love of God for his people, despite their deliberate unfaithfulness that threatened the covenant relationship with God. By contrast, God's faithfulness remained unbroken because of his enduring love. Despite his personal grief, God waited patiently for his love to be returned, so that he could embrace his loved ones and shower upon them the blessings he longed to impart. Such is the love of God for all those with whom he has entered a covenant relationship of love through the precious redeeming blood of the Lord Jesus.

Despite the fact that Hosea gave odd names to his children which seemed to imply that he did not care for them there is strong evidence that he really loved his family and that he actually shared with Gomer in the upbringing of their children. In chapter 11 the prophet draws on his own experience of human fatherhood to express something of the nature of God that had been revealed to him. In this chapter he reaches heights of revelation concerning the love of God that go beyond anything perceived by earlier prophets. In fact, Hosea's words here may have prepared the way for the supreme revelation of the love of God given under the Old Covenant that is found in Isaiah chapters 53 to 55.

God's Love for Israel

Like all the great prophets of Israel, Hosea uses incidents in the history of God's dealings with his covenant people in order to interpret the present. He does so in the context of family life. He hears God saying, *"When Israel was a child, I loved him, and out of Egypt I called my son".*   Hosea 11.1

The emphasis here is looking back to the childhood of the nation and God's tender care in teaching his people and ensuring that they understood his nature and the way he wished to work out his purposes.

God loved his people and watched over them as a father cares for his children. When they were reduced to slavery, through having settled in Egypt instead of simply buying corn and going back to the land God had provided for them, God responded to their cries for help. He raised up Moses in the court of Pharaoh, giving him the ability to communicate with the Egyptian hierarchy, so that when his spiritual training was complete he was able to lead the people out of bondage.

Hosea goes on to highlight the tragedy of Israel's unresponsiveness and their deliberate apostasy. They actually spurned the love of God and all that he had done for them in delivering them from their sufferings in Egypt. Despite all this evidence of God's love for them they had turned their backs upon him. It seemed as though the more God did for them the more they chose to be unfaithful to him. This continued from one generation to the next and the more God spoke to them through the prophets and revealed himself to them, the more they turned away from him.

Even after all God had done to provide for their needs and to protect them in the desert they were still unfaithful to him. He led them into the Promised Land but even there they were unfaithful to him, sacrificing to the local idols; turning to the Baals of the Canaanites in the land he had given to them. But despite their unfaithfulness God had been patient with them for many generations and had watched over them as good parents tenderly watch over their children.

Hosea's Personal Experience

It was at this point that Hosea can be seen drawing on his own experience of family life as well as the pain he had experienced in marriage. In his quiet times in the throne-room of God he had felt something of the pain of God through the unfaithfulness of his people Israel. You can feel the pathos as he wrote what he heard God saying during his times of intercession, *"It was I who taught Ephraim to walk, taking them by the arms; but they did not realise it was I who healed them".*

Hosea 11.3

In his communication with God, Hosea was reminded of his own experience of watching his children in their infancy. He remembered how he and Gomer watched their children take their first faltering steps. When they fell they picked them up and cuddled them, rubbed their bruises and comforted them. As he meditated upon this it was revealed to him that if he could so love his own children, then God the Creator must love his children at least as much as those whom he had created in his own image and a million times more. He realised that God is at least as good and loving as the best and most loving human parent. To say less would be to diminish God. Indeed, the love of God must be millions of times more than the love and compassion of the human beings he has created.

A Difficult Translation

There are considerable translation difficulties with the Hebrew text of the second half of verse 4. The NIV reads *"I led them with cords of human kindness, with ties of love; I lifted the yoke from their neck and bent down to feed them"* Hosea 11.4. There is no agreement among translators and every version of the Bible has a different interpretation of this verse. The Authorised Version reads, *"I drew them with cords of a man, with bands of love: and I was to them as they that take off the yoke on their jaws, and I laid meat unto them."*

The NIV translators have introduced the word 'neck' instead of the literal 'cheek' or 'jaw' in order to try to make sense of it. But it is probably the word 'yoke' that has been mistranslated. If we read 'ul' for 'ol', as in some MSS, we have 'baby' instead of 'yoke'. Literal translation would then be, *'I was to them like those who lift a baby to their cheeks; I bent down to them that I might feed them.'* [2]

---

[2] Some modern translations follow this rendering

Tender Love

This would flow naturally into the image of parental love that the prophet is using to express the tender love of God. He must many times have watched Gomer caring for her babies and noticed the way a young mother catches up her baby when it is distressed. She presses it tenderly to her face to comfort the child and to give physical expression to her love. It is quite likely that Hosea himself did the same thing when comforting one of his children when they were babies. He could feel the response of the infant when pressed against his face. In expressing his own fatherly care he learned something of the Fatherly love of God and his tender care for his children.

Verses 5 and 6 speak of the present situation in the reign of King Hoshea, who reneged on his agreement to pay tribute to the Assyrian Emperor Shalmaneser V and appealed to Egypt for help in driving the Assyrians from his land. Hosea saw this as spelling the end for Ephraim, the northern Kingdom of Israel, because it was rebellion against God who had allowed the Assyrians to dominate them as a judgment on their idolatry.

Apostasy

Instead of accepting their punishment as a rebuke from the Lord, turning back to him in repentance, and waiting patiently for him to deal with the Assyrians, the whole nation had gone farther into apostasy. Instead of crying out to God, they had appealed to a pagan nation for help and were even worshipping the most evil of the pagan gods in order to try to enlist their help.

The term 'Most High' in verse 7 does not refer to God; it is an occult term and refers to the chief of the Baals. But Baal is powerless to rescue them: *'He will by no means exalt them'*. Hosea sees that this apostasy can lead only to further disaster.

Some Israelites had already fled south to Egypt following the revenge wrought by Tiglath-Pileser III in 733 BC when he took over most of Israel's territory. But the prophet saw that even worse was to come: *'Swords will flash in their cities... and put an end to their plans'*.   Hosea 11.6

God's Suffering

In verse 8 Hosea tries to express the inexpressible; the incredible suffering in the heart of God caused by Israel's unfaithfulness. This is the divine dilemma. The case against Israel, God's chosen people with whom he entered into a solemn covenant relationship, had been set out in verses 1 - 7. All that now remained was for God to announce the sentence of punishment that justice demanded.

But instead we are given a picture of Israel, the beloved prodigal son, standing in the presence of his Father and listening to God agonising over what he should do. The law, as given to Moses, stated that a son who persists in stubborn rebellion against his parents should be put to death.[3]

Justice demanded that Israel should be treated like Admah and Zeboiim who were both utterly destroyed along with Sodom and Gomorrah [4]. But the whole of God's compassion was aroused for his errant son whom he had protected, provided for and tenderly cared for since infancy.

God's Unbreakable Love

God's decision is that he will not allow Israel to be completely devastated and utterly destroyed, as they deserve, because he is God and not man; he is the Holy One whose tender love is unending and unbreakable. Even though his people have brought upon themselves disaster and inevitable suffering, God will not cease to love them. He longs for the return of Israel, his prodigal son, whom he will one day restore to himself and resettle in their homeland.   Hosea 11.11

It was here that Hosea received a further tremendous revelation. It was that although God longed to see Israel repent of unfaithfulness and idolatry the salvation of the nation was not dependent upon her repentance but upon God's love.

The salvation of Israel was not conditional upon the moral and spiritual state of the nation. It was entirely dependent upon the love and mercy of God. This was an incredible leap forward in

---

[3] See Deuteronomy 21.18 - 21

[4] See Deuteronomy 29.23

prophetic revelation of the nature of God.

Seven hundred years before the crucifixion of Jesus, Hosea perceived that the basis of our salvation has nothing whatever to do with our righteousness but is rooted entirely in the love and Fatherly forgiveness and compassion of God. In the New Testament this is called the 'grace of God'. Thus the basis for the revelation of God's love in the New Testament was laid through God's self-revelation to his prophets. Their ministry was a vital preparation for the mission of Messiah Jesus.

Centuries after the revelation given to Hosea, the Apostle Paul summarised the outcome of the divine dilemma; God's struggle between the demands of justice that would punish the wicked and his compassion for the weakness of his wayward children. Paul wrote, *'God demonstrates his own love for us in this: while we were still sinners, Christ died for us'.*   Romans 5:8

It is that same inexpressible love of God that has moved the hearts of believers in every generation. As Charles Wesley says in one of his most famous hymns, 'Amazing love, how can it be that Thou my God should die for me?'

It is only God whose love is so great that he can love the unlovable.

Chapter Three

GOD'S LOVE FOR THE DEPRESSED

This chapter has messages from both Isaiah and Jeremiah that reveal the amazing power of the unbreakable love of God to dispel depression, drive out bitterness and set people free from despair.

Love and Rebuke

It is surprising how often love and rebuke go together in God's dealings with his people just as they do with a loving parent. The mother whose child runs into the road, and is dramatically rescued by a passer-by, receives him back, snatched from the jaws of death, and immediately begins to scold him severely. Love and rebuke are mixed in her response.

So often in the Bible we find the same mixture in the expression of God's love for his people although the rebuke is much more of a regret expressing God's pain that people have not understood his love or responded lovingly to him.

In Isaiah 50:1-3, there is a beautiful example of God scolding his people in love. *'This is what the Lord says; "Where is your mother's certificate of divorce with which I sent her away? Or to which of my creditors did I sell you? Because of your sins you were sold; because of your transgressions your mother was sent away. When I came, why was there no-one? When I called, why was there no-one to answer? Was my arm too short to ransom you? Do I lack the strength to rescue you? By a mere rebuke I dry up the sea, I turn rivers into a desert; their fish rot for lack of water and die of thirst. I clothe the sky with darkness and make sackcloth its covering."'*

Unheeded Warnings

The message of this passage needs to be understood in the context of the exile in Babylon, where thousands of the tribe of Judah had been taken into slavery following the fall of Jerusalem in 586 BC. The destruction of the city had been clearly foretold by Jeremiah but his warnings had gone unheeded. The people had believed the false prophets who said that God would never allow Jerusalem to fall into enemy hands or the Temple to be destroyed.

With the exception of Jeremiah, prophets and priests alike had been prepared to turn a blind eye to the idolatry that was everywhere in the land, and to the adultery, violence and bloodshed which characterised a generation that had rejected the word of God. There were altars to pagan gods on every street corner in Jerusalem. The rich exploited the poor and injustice and corruption were everywhere to be seen. If there was a dispute between two families, one rich and one poor and it went to court, the rich man would bribe the judge and the poor man would be denied justice. Everything in the social, economic and religious life of the nation was contrary to the word of God, which Jeremiah saw as a recipe for national disaster.

Temple Sermon

In his famous 'temple sermon'[1] - a message which had to be spoken *outside the temple* because the prophet was banned by the priests - Jeremiah identified six sins of Jerusalem which, he said, would lead to the destruction of the city unless there was repentance. Jeremiah said that God would remove his cover of protection from an unholy and unrighteous city.

The six sins were:-

false religion,

oppression,

injustice,

violence,

idolatry,

immorality.

Jeremiah 7.4 - 9

He had concluded his message with a warning that God was watching! He said that the Lord had spoken to them again and again but they had refused to listen. God had called but they had not answered. Therefore he would thrust them from his presence just as he had done with their brothers the people of the northern kingdom of Israel that had been conquered by the Assyrians.

---

[1] See Jeremiah 7.1 - 15

It is a matter of history that Jeremiah's warnings went unheeded, the city was conquered and its leading citizens were taken into slavery in Babylon.

Spirit of Despair

The generation of those deported to Babylon was destined to die in slavery as aliens in a foreign land. But their offspring were the children of promise who would see the prophecies of restoration fulfilled. There was, however, a major stumbling block – depression and despair.

The exhausting one thousand mile trek in chains from Jerusalem to Babylon was an experience none of the exiles would ever forget. Their last sight of Jerusalem was of the city in flames, with enemy soldiers still presiding over the final acts of destruction. They really had never believed that God would allow Jerusalem to be destroyed by an enemy and they saw it as a terrible punishment from God for their sins. Their sense of failure and rejection by God brought upon them a wave of spiritual depression that is reflected in Psalm 137, *'By the waters of Babylon we sat and wept when we remembered Zion... How can we sing the songs of the Lord while in a foreign land?'*

This depression was communicated to their children and the prophet saw this as a major stumbling block to God being able to fulfil his good purposes of restoration and return to the land. The time of restoration was now very near but they were unable to receive the good news because they were too depressed. Their faith in God had to be renewed. Until their confidence in God was restored they were unable to receive a message from him. The reality of the power of the enemy was all around them in Babylon and they had forgotten the great things that God had done for their forefathers in the past. They were so immersed in depression that they could not think clearly.

Depression

Depression is a favourite ploy of the enemy to frustrate God's purposes and to blind us to God's good plans for our lives. Most Christians, at some time in their lives, go through a time of depression. If we suffer a severe setback in our plans, things don't turn out as we expect, we don't pass an important exam, or we don't get the job we expected, we feel a strong sense of failure and bewilderment, we don't know what to do next and our whole outlook on life becomes depressed. Depression can also be brought on by the actions of others such as when someone we trusted lets us down; we feel betrayed and think we will never trust anyone again. Our outlook on life is coloured by this experience and disappointment can turn either to depression or to anger and bitterness.

In my pastoral ministry I've officiated at many weddings, most of which have been very happy occasions with radiant brides and nervous grooms, but there was one wedding that stands out in my memory. The bride was a lovely young lady, in her 20s, marrying a young man some two or three years older. They were both university graduates and in professional occupations. I had been getting to know them quite well over the previous six months so I knew that the bride had a complicated family history but even so two weeks before the wedding I was quite startled when she asked me about our security arrangements. "What do you mean?" I enquired. She then asked if we had any strong men available who could handle violence if there was any trouble at her wedding.

A Family Dispute

By this time I was positively alarmed and I said that I needed to know exactly what she had in mind and what she was afraid might happen. The ensuing explanation was long and complicated revealing a great deal of pain through broken family relationships. Her father had left home some years earlier and had not supported her mother or his children since then. But the bride had recently been in touch with her father and she had actually invited him to give her away at her wedding.

This resulted in a sharp dispute with her mother and they had not spoken for some weeks. She said that her mother wanted her current partner to give her away and she would be extremely angry if her ex-husband came to the wedding with the woman for whom he had left her. The bride said that her mother sometimes gave way to displays of violent anger and she feared that this might happen at the wedding.

After some discussion I asked if her mother was coming to the wedding rehearsal the following week. She said that she was intending to come. I said that after the rehearsal I would arrange to see her mother alone. She duly came the following Saturday and the rehearsal went through without any traumatic incident. Eventually I sat down alone with her mother. She was surprisingly open and talked freely about her life after her husband left her for another woman and the financial hardships and emotional difficulties she had suffered as a single mother in maintaining and supporting her two children through school and university.

Inevitably she felt strong resentment towards her ex-husband who had not contributed any financial support or shown any interest in his children. She had felt very much alone. Her daughter had always wanted to see her father as she had missed him throughout her childhood. When she was 18 she had contacted him and arranged to meet at a particular venue but he failed to turn up. She had been bitterly disappointed and her mother now deeply resented his willingness to come and participate in her daughter's wedding after the despicable way he had behaved in the past.

Holding Resentment

I could do no other than agree with her that she was totally justified in feeling that his behaviour did not warrant his presence at the wedding. I was able, in all sincerity, to say what a lovely daughter she had produced and this was a great tribute to her. She had overcome all the difficulties and given her daughter love and security to bring her to this point in her life. After some further conversation about her life since she had been deserted by her husband I said that it appeared that the greatest cost was in her own peace of mind.

She was carrying a deep resentment that had grown into bitterness over the years and this must have affected her outlook on life and her relationships with others. She agreed. So I then asked if she would like to be free from that spirit of bitterness and she said that she would like it more than anything. I talked to her about the love of God and what Jesus had done for us to break the power of the kind of spirit that was troubling her. I said that she could be free in an instant if she would allow me to pray for her. She agreed with surprising eagerness. Five minutes later she was free.

Freedom from Bitterness

A week later we had one of the most amazing and joyful weddings I've ever known. The groom arrived early so I was able to talk to him before everyone else arrived. He was a different man. A week ago he'd been quite gloomy and apprehensive. Now he was radiant and he couldn't stop talking about the things that had happened during the week, of how his bride and her mother had been reconciled and the whole atmosphere in the house was different.

His future mother-in-law was totally changed. There had been no anger; only smiles and happiness. Despite all the pressures of the final week and the many things to do in preparation for the wedding the whole atmosphere had been light and happy. All the signs of depression and bitterness had disappeared.

The actual wedding was one of the happiest I've ever conducted and the bride's mother was actually able to meet the man she had not seen for many years who had hurt her so deeply. She was even able to greet the woman who had replaced her in his affections. Clearly she was drawing her strength from the Lord who had so wonderfully lifted her burden.

It was easy to talk about the transforming love of God in my message to the couple and they knew exactly what was meant when I quoted Paul saying, *"If anyone is in Christ, he is a new creation; the old has gone, the new has come!"* 2 Corinthians 5.17. I had not, in fact, asked any strong men to be present, although I had arranged for a group of intercessors to be on the premises. There was much joy among them that their prayers were answered.

Moses and Divorce

It was that kind of radical change of mindset that Isaiah was longing to see in the exiles in Babylon where there was not only widespread despair but a type of communal hopelessness. Even the healthy young men among the exiles were saying, 'Our parents were rejected by God and we are children who have been sold into slavery.' The prophet countered this strongly by reminding them of their Hebrew customs.

Only men could divorce their spouses in those days and a man would sometimes say in anger that he was divorcing his wife after a heated dispute. But because of the seriousness of such an action for the stability of family life in the nation, Moses had insisted that it should be put in writing. The divorce was not final until the man had actually written out a certificate of divorce and had it witnessed by the elders of the community.

The prophet declared that God had never made the divorce final. God's love for his people was so great that he would never finally reject them, even though in anger he thrust them from his presence because of their wilful rejection of him. Even though they broke their part of the covenant, he himself would never break his covenant vows.

The accusation that God had sold his children into slavery was scornfully rejected. God was not like a bankrupt man who was forced to sell his children in order to settle his debts to his creditors. Who were God's creditors? Did they really imagine God to be bankrupt? The reason why God withdrew his cover over Jerusalem and allowed the enemy to destroy the city and take the people into slavery was entirely because they had rejected God.

This is spelt out clearly, *"Because of your sins you were sold; because of your transgressions your mother was sent away"* Isaiah 50.1. This should come as no surprise to the people. The bitter experience of exile had given them plenty of time to reflect upon the sins that had brought about the national disaster. Surely the evidence that the people had rejected the word of God and the warnings brought by Jeremiah were so clear that no one could be left in any doubt.

Countering Despair

The prophet's task, however, was not to rub salt into the wound but to counter the fatalism and despair that had replaced faith in God. Most of the people were well aware that they deserved all they got and knew that they had brought the disaster upon themselves. But now God was calling to them and no-one was there to answer him; no-one was listening. Their spiritual depression was so deep; they had ceased to believe that God had the power to save them by rescuing them from the plight into which they had been plunged.

Many of the older people had so firmly embraced the lesson of the exile - that sin brings inevitable consequences - that they had ceased to believe that God could reverse the outcome of their sin and bring redemption to those who so fully deserved their punishment! Among the younger exiles, born in Babylon, there was evidence of the acceptance of the local culture which included taking part in the pagan religious festivals and the prophet accuses them of walking in torchlight processions which was a disgrace to the faith of their forefathers[1]. But this was all an outcome of the loss of faith and the despair that had overwhelmed the whole expatriate community.

The message the prophet brought to counter the spiritual depression of the people was to ask if they thought that God's arm was too short to reach out to Babylon and ransom them from slavery. *'Do I lack the strength to rescue you?'* God asked through the prophet, and then reminded them, *'By a mere rebuke I dry up the sea, I turn rivers into a desert.'*   Isaiah 50.2

The one who was speaking to them was none other than the Creator of the Universe, who held all things in his hands. He had the power to change the natural order of creation by his word, and he also had the power to change the natural order of the moral law in order to fulfil his promise to his people.

This was a major step in the revelation of the nature of God. He was not only the God of the little nation of Israel, he was actually the Lord of Creation and Governor of the Universe who held the nations in his hands.

God Dispels the Darkness

The unbreakable love of God is seen in this passage as he moves to dispel the dark clouds of despair and depression which hung over his people, reassuring them that he is a God of salvation who never totally rejects his people however much they may have sinned; just as parents continue to love their children however wayward they are; loving them even when their own love is spurned.

God's love for us, his children, is a million times greater than that of even the best of human parents. He knows our circumstances and even when we have brought difficulties upon ourselves through our own foolishness or sin he never ceases to love us. Sometimes God has to shake us in order to pull us out of our

---

[1] See Isaiah 50.11

depression just as whole nations were shaken through the financial crisis that began in 2008 with the collapse of many banks and great financial institutions.

God sometimes has to shake the nations in order to emphasise his loving warnings that we are heading for disaster. This is expressed in Isaiah 26.9 - 10, *"When your judgements come upon the earth, the people of the world learn righteousness. Though grace is shown to the wicked they do not learn righteousness, they go on doing evil and regard not the majesty of the Lord."*

When God moves to shake the world it is not only nations that are shaken but also millions of individuals, which include the righteous as well as the unrighteous. But God always reassures those who are in a covenant relationship with him. He will never forsake us and he has good plans for our lives. Through his reassurances and the experience of his love he lifts us out of depression and despair and enables us to move into the blessings of his promises to enjoy being restored to the joy of a close walk with our God.

Unbreakable *Love*

Chapter Four

GOD'S LOVE FOR THE WEAK AND POWERLESS

This chapter examines the way the Prophets discovered the unbreakable love of God, his special love for the weak and powerless, and how his love builds them up and strengthens them, transforming their lives.

Revealing God

It cannot be overemphasised that the primary task of the great prophets of Israel was to reveal the nature and purposes of God. Of course, they had to serve the people of their generation, which meant dealing with current issues and giving guidance to the leaders of the nation in accordance with the word of God. But the prophets were men and women who had learned to get into the presence of the Almighty God and enjoy a personal relationship with him.

It was through this personal relationship that the prophets came to understand the amazing love of God for all people and the special love he had for those whom he had called to be in a covenant relationship and through whom he could reveal his nature and purposes to the world. It was as each of the prophets of Israel grew in the quality of their relationship with God, that their knowledge of him grew. This is rather like the intimacy of marriage. In a really happy marriage, when a man and woman have been together in a love union for many years, they reach the stage where they almost know what each is thinking before it is expressed in words.

Similarly a close relationship with God over many years enabled the prophets to know the thoughts of God. God has not changed so that close relationship is available to us today. In fact, through Jesus our Lord it should be easier to know the Father. The prophets were pioneers exploring roads first travelled by the patriarchs from the time of Abraham. This calling to take the Word of God to the nations of Israel drove them to new depths of intimacy in their relationship with God. Through this relationship

God was able to reveal himself to each of the prophets.

The Book of Isaiah has a very special place in expressing this revelation and in chapter 54, part of which is reproduced on page 63, we reach a high point in the understanding of God's love.

Isaiah Chapters 40 to 55[1] deal with the exiles of Judah living under slavery in Babylon in the last few years of the exile when the message God was sending was intended to prepare them for the return to Jerusalem. Isaiah's first task had been to convince the exiles that the God of their forefathers Abraham, Isaac and Jacob was no other than the Creator of the Universe, the one and only true God.

The covenant God had originally made with Abraham was still valid. Even though Israel had broken their side of the covenant by idolatry, immorality and ignoring the warnings God had sent to them through the prophets he, nevertheless, was faithful to keep his covenant promises. God had heard the cries of his people and seen their suffering and was now about to overthrow Babylon and restore his people to the land he had promised to their forefathers. He was about to redeem them from slavery.

God Keeps his Promise

The message of Chapter 54 builds on the previous chapters that established the fact that God has the ability to fulfil his promises. The prophet now has to convince the people that despite their unworthiness God will do as he promises because he loves them. For all those who for any reason feel their own personal unworthiness this is a very special message.

The message starts with the exhortation to sing and to shout for joy. The slave community in Babylon were like a woman who was unable to have children. In those days it was seen as a disgrace for a woman to be childless and this was usually ascribed to God having deliberately withheld his blessing. Abraham and Sarah both believed this, but God promised that they would have a child despite Sarah's age and their son Isaac was seen as a child of promise in contrast to the child Abraham had fathered through Hagar. Hannah, the mother of Samuel, was also thought to be barren but when God answered her prayer she was overwhelmed

---

[1] see footnote on page 36

in thanksgiving to God. In her prayer Hannah recognised the sovereignty of God, *"The Lord sends poverty and wealth, he humbles and he exalts. He raises the poor from the dust and lifts the needy from the ash heap".*   I Samuel 2.7

Isaiah may well have had Hannah's prayer in his mind when he brought this word of encouragement to the exiles in Babylon. They are told to burst into song and shout for joy like a barren woman discovering that she was carrying a child. Of course, the exiles were not yet released from slavery but God expects his people to respond to his love with trust and when he promises to do something they can be certain that he will fulfil his promise so they can begin celebrating the moment they hear the promise. That is the kind of faith God expects from his people, especially those who feel lonely, or that their lives are barren. When God gives a promise you can begin to live in expectation, which changes your whole outlook on life.

A Preacher in China

Our first visit to China was memorable. Monica and I and our team from London were staying with Jackie Pullinger in Hong Kong where she had an amazing ministry among young drug addicts. We had been doing a mission in her community, teaching on the message of the Prophets and the gifts of the Holy Spirit. Jackie had arranged for us to meet with leaders of underground churches in Mainland China. One of the outstanding leaders who had suffered much for his faith was Pastor Samuel Lam.

It was an unforgettable experience to have the privilege of sitting in the home of this amazing man of God and listen to his story told with quiet gentle humility. We were in Guangzhou, the capital of Canton Province in the People's Republic of China in the days before China began to open up to the West. We asked Pastor Lam how he had survived 22 years in prison under Mao Tse Tung's repressive regime. His first prison sentence for preaching the gospel had been two years but when he still continued to preach he was given a further unlimited sentence which actually lasted 20 years. Throughout that time he did not know when he would be released but God had promised that the day would come when he would once again pastor a congregation and be free to preach the word of the Lord.

His wife died while he was in prison so he never saw her again.

Although he did not know when he would be released, he knew that he would not die in prison, but there were many times that he was near to death through the cruelty of the guards and the rough treatment that he received. God had given him a promise and he held on to that promise knowing that it would be fulfilled.

Samuel suffered many punishments for preaching the gospel to his fellow prisoners but nothing stopped him. After he was badly injured by a runaway train down the coalmine where he was working, the guards gave him a new job. He could no longer do the hard work at the coalface so he was made the Camp Barber. He saw this as evidence of the grace and mercy of God who had now provided him with a 'pulpit' in the prison from which he could preach the word of the Lord. Every prisoner came to sit in his chair and as he snipped their hair he whispered the gospel in their ears. He spoke about the love of God and how he had sent Jesus to be our Saviour. Many lives were changed through the word that he gave to the prisoners.

After Mao's death he was released from prison and allowed to go back to his home town where he began teaching English. Within a few months his first three pupils gave their lives to Jesus and that was the beginning of his church. Seven years later he had baptised 900 people; 300 had gone out as missionaries and church planters all over China. The word of the Lord was spreading across the land from this one man who had believed God's promise for 20 years even though everything was against him.

Inspiring Faith

It was this quality of faith that Isaiah was seeking to inspire among the exiles in Babylon many of whom had been born into slavery and did not know if they would ever be given their freedom. Before the fall of Jerusalem, Jeremiah had been given a promise from God that one day they would be restored to the land of their forefathers. This promise had seemed more and more remote as the years passed and a kind of hopeless despair grew among the people to whom Isaiah ministered.

He reminded them of the days when their ancestors lived in the desert after their release from slavery in Egypt. In those days they lived in tents and it was the women of the community who were responsible for the family tent; as the family increased so they would enlarge the tent by adding another room. This was done by stretching out the side curtain to extend the roof and adding another side to it. With each extension, the cords of the tent had to be lengthened and stronger tent pegs had to be driven in to the ground to take the additional weight.

Isaiah was saying to the people that the day of their release from Babylon was drawing close and they had a long trek ahead of them when they would be living in tents but God intended blessing them and prospering the community, as he had done throughout the forty years in the wilderness. So this was the message he proclaimed:

"Sing, O barren woman, you who never bore a child; burst into song, shout for joy, you who were never in labour; because more are the children of the desolate woman than of her who has a husband, says the Lord.

"Enlarge the place of your tent, stretch your tent curtains wide, do not hold back; lengthen your cords, strengthen your stakes. For you will spread out to the right and to the left, your descendants will dispossess nations and settle in their desolate cities.

"Do not be afraid; you will not suffer shame. Do not fear disgrace; you will not be humiliated. You will forget the shame of your youth and remember no more the reproach of your widowhood. For your Maker is your husband - the Almighty is his name - the Holy One of Israel is your Redeemer; he is called the God of all the earth.

"For a brief moment I abandoned you, but with deep compassion I will bring you back, in a surge of anger I hid my face from you for a moment, but with everlasting kindness I will have compassion on you says the Lord your Redeemer."

Isaiah 54.1-8

Enlarge and Stretch

In faith, Isaiah could already see the captives being released and God's promised overthrow of Babylon being fulfilled because he knew that God always keeps his promises; so he brings this message, *"Enlarge the place of your tent, stretch your tent curtains wide, do not hold back; lengthen your cords, strengthen your stakes."* The message is given with a sense of urgency so there are four verbs, all in the imperative case -

Enlarge! Stretch! Lengthen! Strengthen!

Soon this message will need to be literally obeyed but now it has a spiritual interpretation. Enlarge your vision! Stretch your expectation! Lengthen your trust! Strengthen your faith! Then you will be ready to respond positively the very moment God opens the door and sets you free from the shackles of Babylon.

A generation earlier Jeremiah had warned the people of Jerusalem to prepare for exile, *"Gather up your belongings to leave the land, you who live under siege"* Jeremiah 10.17. In the same passage he foresaw the people lamenting, *"My tent is destroyed, all its ropes are destroyed"* Jeremiah 10.20. Now Isaiah was foreseeing an amazing reversal of this, because God was restoring his blessing to Israel and the nation was moving into a time of prosperity, *"Enlarge the place of your tent, do not hold back!"* Isaiah 54.2

Living in Victory

Despite the attractiveness of the message the people found it hard to accept. Sometimes we find it hard to accept good news; we get so saturated with bad news. Every day the newspapers are full of it so we come to expect bad news; we become conditioned to it and we cease to expect good news. This is the point of real danger because **blessing** is the **normal environment** in which God's people should be living *even when in Babylon*.

During the 20 years' imprisonment that Pastor Samuel Lam lived under the cruel repressive regime of the slave camp, the guards were unable to break him because he was living in the Kingdom. When they took away his Bible and burned it in front of him they were still unable to break his spirit. He saved any scraps of paper that came his way and from memory he wrote the whole of John's Gospel, Romans and a number of the Psalms. So he produced his own Bible from which he ministered to other prisoners whenever he had opportunities.

Pastor Lam proved that even when you are living in Babylon you do not have to allow your mind to be dominated by the spirit or values of Babylon. Kingdom people can live in the Kingdom even under slavery! This is how many of the gospel songs and spirituals were born among African Christians in the Caribbean islands 200 years ago.

It was this 'Kingdom' spirit that Isaiah was seeking to establish when he brought the promise of God, *"For you will spread out to the right and to the left; your descendants will dispossess nations and settle in their desolate cities."*   Isaiah 54.3

A similar promise had been given to Jacob, *"I will give you and your descendants the land on which you are lying. Your descendants will be like the dust of the earth, and you will spread out to the west and to the east, to the north and to the south. All peoples on earth will be blessed through you and your offspring".*   Genesis 28.13-14

Promise of Blessing

God had fulfilled the promise to give the land to the descendants of Jacob whom he renamed 'Israel' but due to their rebellion God had allowed the land to be given over to the Babylonians. Now he was making a promise to the remnant of his people that he would restore the land to them so that the promise to Jacob that their descendants would increase and spread out across the whole world would one day be fulfilled. So too is the promise that the people of all nations will be blessed through them.

That promise is still being fulfilled today. The people of Israel have indeed been scattered across the whole world and the good news brought through Jesus the Messiah is still being spread across the nations. But it must have been hard for that tiny company of ex-patriots to comprehend the magnitude of what they were hearing through the prophet Isaiah.

It is very probable that Isaiah himself did not understand it, but he was a faithful messenger of God, declaring in public what he had heard in private: bringing to the people the word of the Lord that he had received from the throne of God. As if to reinforce the cast-iron certainty of the promise of God he added, *"Do not be afraid; you will not suffer shame. Do not fear disgrace; you will not be humiliated. You will forget the shame of your youth and remember no more of the reproach of your widowhood".*   Isaiah 54.4

Time after time Isaiah had to repeat the promises of God, which shows the depths of despair into which the people had sunk. The "shame of your youth" probably referred to the time Israel was enslaved in Egypt, while the "reproach of your widowhood" no doubt referred to the exile in Babylon. During both of these times of suffering people were powerless to save themselves. God had to rescue his people; redeeming them from slavery. The promise is here reinforced that their humiliation would be removed and all nations would recognise what God had done for his people.

Covenant Promises

Isaiah then makes an astonishing statement. He says *"For your Maker is your husband - the Lord Almighty is his name - the Holy One of Israel is your Redeemer; he is called the God of all the earth".* Isaiah 54.5. The God of Israel who is also the Creator of the Universe was going to enter into a new relationship with his people in order to fulfil the promises of the covenant. The remnant of the nation in Babylon must have been at least 59,000 [2]. Jeremiah says that a total of 4,600 people [3] were taken from Jerusalem to Babylon over a 14 year period, 596 BC to 582 BC.

Assuming that Isaiah was speaking a few years before the overthrow of Babylon by Cyrus in 539 BC many of the first generation would have already died but in the fifty years since 596 BC [4] the exile population had multiplied. They were a significant community and many were prosperous with their own servants. [5] Clearly they had obeyed Jeremiah's instructions in the early days of the exile before the destruction of Jerusalem, *"Marry and have sons and daughters; find wives for your sons and give your daughters in marriage, so that they too may have sons and daughters. Increase in number there; do not decrease."*

Jeremiah 29.6

God was now going to be in a special relationship with his covenant people. He was going to do something new, as he had already promised, *"Forget the former things; do not dwell on the past. See, I'm going to do a new thing!"* Isaiah 43.18. Instead of Israel being like a widow or like *"a wife deserted and distressed in spirit",* God was going to be a husband to the nation raising a new people who would take his word to all nations in the world and be a light for the Gentiles.

Isaiah was reminding the people that the God of their forefathers who was known as "The Holy One of Israel" was coming to act as

---

[2] Ezra 2.64 records the families returning after the exile with a total number of 42,360. We know that not all the exiles returned at this time.

[3] See Jeremiah 52.30

[4] This was the date of the first wave of exiles to be taken to Babylon

[5] See Ezra 2.64

their Redeemer, to release them from slavery in Babylon. Their Lord and Maker would pay the redemption price for their freedom. He alone had the power to do this because he was "The God of all the earth". He was the one who held the destiny of the nations in his hands and before him the mighty power of Babylon was as nothing. It was he who was promising to set his people free and he was not only faithful to keep his promises, but he had the power to do so.

Blessing the Powerless

God loves to bless his people and especially those who feel powerless. He loves to surprise those who don't know him or who fell far away, having made a mess of their lives. During our ministry in the East End of London I was in the church hall one evening when a gang from another neighbourhood raided our youth club. I went in to try to sort things out while the leader rang the police. The knives came out and things began to look a bit ugly, when the sound of sirens outside caused a rush for the exits that were soon blocked by some large policemen looking very businesslike.

In the ensuing chaos I noticed one lad who had been coming to our youth club for several weeks and was certainly not one of the invaders. He was being marched outside by a burly sergeant who, by the time I got there, had got him spread-eagled over the bonnet of a police car. I am normally very respectful to anyone in authority but I felt a sudden surge of indignation that this lad whom I knew had a troubled past was being summarily arrested.

The young man came from a dysfunctional family and was well known to the police. Now he was being picked up when he was innocent of causing the disturbance in our hall. I immediately addressed the sergeant with unusual boldness; "You let him go!" I demanded. "He's not one of the gang who came in to cause trouble. He's a good lad!" The policeman was probably even more astonished at my outburst than I was! Without another word he let him go and strode back into the hall looking for some other villain. I saw this young man again a few days later and he got as near as possible to thanking me. It was probably the first time in his life anyone had spoken up for him and he was clearly moved by the experience. Someone actually trusted him, and it wasn't long before he became one of the leaders in our youth club and his whole life turned around as he responded to the gospel. There are so many people today who feel powerless and unloved, especially those who have been hurt through family breakdown; the deserted wife, or the children whose mother takes them to live with another man whom they hate, or the young people who are taken from one foster home to another but never feel secure in anyone's love.

Community Laments

Isaiah was dealing with a whole community like this. The book of Lamentations has vivid descriptions of the distress of the survivors of the Jerusalem Holocaust. *"The roads to Zion mourn for no-one comes to her appointed feasts. All her gateways are desolate, her priests groan, her maidens grieve, and she is in anguish"* Lamentations 1.4. To make things even more bitter the whole nation believed that it was God who had brought this disaster upon his own people because of their sins. *"Her foes have become her masters; her enemies are at ease. The Lord has brought her grief because of her many sins"* Lamentations 1.5. In lament after lament the same belief is expressed, *"Is it nothing to you, all you who pass by? Look around and see. Is any suffering like my suffering that was inflicted on me, that the Lord brought on me in the day of his fierce anger?"* Lamentations 1.12

Many of these 'community laments' express bitterness towards God. While acknowledging his justice in punishing them for their sinfulness, the horror of what had been done by the enemy was so great that it seemed unbelievable that God would have allowed such a disaster to happen. *"Young and old lie together in the dust of the streets; my young men and maidens have fallen by the sword. You have slain them in the day of your anger; you have slaughtered them without pity".* Lamentations 2.21

Did God really intend such a thing to happen? Had God completely abandoned them? Surely a God of love would not wipe them out completely? They argued it out among themselves. *"Because of the Lord's great love we are not consumed, for his compassions never fail, they are new every morning; great is your faithfulness... for men are not cast off by the Lord for ever. Though he brings grief, he will show compassion, so great is his unfailing love. For he does not willingly bring affliction or grief to the children of men".* Lamentations 3.22 - 33

God's Everlasting Kindness

It was against this background of mixed emotions in the Jewish community in Babylon that Isaiah was ministering. He used what people were saying in these community discussions and brought a direct word from God, *"For a brief moment I abandoned you, but with deep compassion I will bring you back. In a surge of anger I hid my face from you for a moment, but with everlasting kindness I will have compassion on you, says the Lord your Redeemer"* Isaiah 54.7-8. These two verses are among the most beautiful words in the Bible for revealing the heart of God. He had withdrawn his cover of protection over his people but now, his everlasting kindness and compassion were deeply moving him to come to their rescue.

If the people were going to be ready to respond to the call to return to Jerusalem after the overthrow of Babylon they had to be reassured of the love of God for them and that, despite the tragedy he had allowed to happen, he had by no means abrogated his covenant responsibilities. He was a God of faithfulness, compassion and love. He was longing to pour out his blessings upon his beloved people. If they would now put their trust in him he would not only crush the Babylonian Empire and release his people, but he would also give them the strength to go back to Jerusalem and rebuild the towns and cities of Judah. A time of restoration and great prosperity lay ahead of them but these blessings were dependent upon their faith and their willingness to trust the Lord their God.

Corporate Responsibility

Among the exiles in Babylon there must have been many who had not practised idolatry, but had kept themselves clean in order to love and serve the Lord. Yet they also suffered the same fate as the idolaters and adulterers. They suffered because of the corporate state of the nation. This always presents a problem for believers. Jesus refers to this problem when he says that God *"causes his sun to rise on the evil and the good, and sends rain on the righteous and the unrighteous"* Matthew 5.45. When one person in a family sins, it can affect all members of the family. When a nation is attacked by an enemy the whole nation is at war and the righteous as well as the unrighteous are likely to suffer. When the banking crisis of 2008 spread across the world it was caused by a relatively small number of individuals whose avaricious and corrupt practices brought down great financial institutions. But it was not only the greedy bankers who suffered; millions of ordinary people lost their jobs and were plunged into despair as they unsuccessfully searched for work and were left to join the mounting dole queues.

It may not seem fair that the innocent suffer with the guilty but we have to learn the hard lessons of corporate responsibility; that our actions affect other people. No man is an island and God created us to live in families and communities and nations where we have to recognise our responsibilities to each other. It was a very hard lesson for Israel to learn. Jeremiah warned them for 40 years before the Babylonians finally destroyed the city of Jerusalem. Clearly, both the leaders and the people had never understood the nature and purposes of God. As the Babylonian army drew closer, instead of the whole nation coming together in prayer to seek God as they had done when the Assyrians invaded more than 100 years earlier and the nation was led by the righteous King Hezekiah, they became more and more idolatrous and made themselves abhorrent to God. They set up altars to other gods on the streets of Jerusalem invoking all the pagan gods in their desperation [6].

God's Everlasting Love

In reaction, God had removed his cover of protection over the ity but now he was expressing his compassion and his love. Israel had to learn that God could feel anger and pain and love just as we can because he has made us human beings in his own image. That is the nature of a personal God. He was not like the impersonal gods of wood and stone. But, because he is a personal God, he feels grief and extreme displeasure when his beloved people deliberately turn their backs upon him, although his anger only lasts a moment.

In order to understand the nature of God, that statement has to be repeated – his anger only lasts a moment. But his love lasts forever and ever. His love lasts forever and ever!

The Hebrew word used here and translated in the NIV as *'everlasting kindness'* is 'hesed'. It is a beautiful word that can also be translated 'unbreakable love' or 'everlasting love'.

---

[6] See Jeremiah 7.17

It is used by the prophets to describe the indescribable love of God. There is no word in any language that is capable of doing justice to a description of the love of God.

We are attempting to use finite human language to describe the infinite nature of the personal God who so loved the world and so longed to be in a personal love relationship with his human children whom he had created in his own image - capable of responding to his love and entering into a unique personal relationship with him - that he had to find a way of dealing with our sinful human nature that was blocking the personal relationship.

God's way was through self-sacrifice; coming in human flesh as our Saviour and Redeemer, paying the redemption price himself to set us free. John expresses this in theological language, *"The Word became flesh and made his dwelling among us"* John 1.14. And Paul says, *"God was reconciling the world to himself in Christ, not counting men's sins against them"*. 2 Corinthians 5.19

God is Love

The difficulty we face in speaking about the love of God is that we are not simply dealing with **an attribute** of God; we are trying to describe his **very nature**. In the First Letter of John, the Apostle appeals to Christians to love each other because love comes from God. He says, *"Everyone who loves has been born of God and knows God. Whoever does not love does not know God, because God is love"*. 1 John 4.7 - 8

This astounding statement is repeated in verse 16 where it is further amplified. *"God is love. Whoever lives in love lives in God, and God in him."* This is closely linked with Jesus' teaching in the Fourth Gospel where he commands the disciples to love one another. He says *"I am in the Father and the Father is in me"* John 14.11. He also says, *"I am in my Father, and you are in me, and I am in you"*. John 14.20

Love One Another

These statements are an attempt to put into words the astonishing truth that when we accept the Lordship of Jesus in our lives he actually dwells within us. That is his promise, *"If anyone loves me, he will obey my teaching. My Father will love him, and we will come to him and make our home with him"*. John 14.23. That means a permanent residence: not just an overnight stay!

Jesus, as the embodiment of the love of God actually lives within those who have put their lives into his hands and his presence is demonstrated to others through his love being seen in our lifestyles and actions - *"By this all men will know that you are my disciples, if you love one another".*

John 3.35

This is how God intends his work to be done in the world. But of even more importance - it is through us, his people, that he reveals himself to the world.

Chapter Five

GOD'S LOVE FOR THE BROKEN

This chapter deals with the promise of God's enduring and unbreakable love which is the prelude to the announcement of a paradigm shift in world history – the re-building of Jerusalem in preparation for the coming of Messiah, which is also a sign of God's unbreakable and transforming love for all his children.

The secular world simply does not understand faith! This was brought home to us forcefully when we were negotiating with a firm of developers for the acquisition of Moggerhanger Park.

A Faith Project

During our ministry in London God had given us a promise that he would give us a place outside London to develop the ministry. We had to wait about ten years before the time was right for God to fulfil his promise. Then we were very clearly guided to the place in Bedfordshire which became our ministry base. The property was in an uninhabitable semi-derelict condition. It was a listed Georgian house that the developers had been unable to adapt for commercial purposes as they had hoped.

The County Conservation Officer was insisting that they carry out essential repairs, so they offered to give[1] the house to us on condition that we carried out the full programme of repairs which they estimated would cost £350,000. We agreed to do this but they wanted a guarantee of our ability to carry out the repairs. did not have any money in our budget for such a capital expenditure but we said that we were Christians and we believed that God would supply all that was needed.

They were not impressed with this and preferred a letter from the bank manager saying that we had £350,000 in our account!

---

[1] God's promise was to 'give' us a ministry base. This was quite literally fulfilled although to complete the legal transfer of the property to Harvest Vison (the trust we set up) we were charged £1.00. The house is now worth £7 million which we call "kingdom economics"!

Of course, we could not supply such a letter but there was no way they would change their minds. In the event we wrote to all our prayer partners stating the situation and saying that we believed there would be that amount of money in our account by the end of the month.

Our prayer partners clearly caught the vision and listened to what the Lord was saying to them with the result that by the end of the month there was not £350,000 but £500,000 in the account! The extra money was the exact amount that we needed to purchase the other buildings linked with the house and to secure the whole estate for the ministry. This was a clear sign of God's blessing upon the project.

Kingdom Values

This was only the beginning of the enormous venture upon which we embarked but we all saw it as a confirmation of God's promise that he would give us a base for the ministry outside London and that he would use it for his purposes to bring honour and glory to his name. The little battle with the developers was just the beginning of the clash between the values of the Kingdom and values of the world.

It was Jerusalem and Babylon played out in the contemporary scene, but it was also a small demonstration of the absolute certainty of God's promises being fulfilled. Once you know that you have received a word from God with a promise, and when that word has been confirmed, it is a cast-iron guarantee. The world may not recognise it as such, but believers are able to stand on such a promise and to know that they will not be ashamed when they take actions based on a promise given by the Lord.

It was this kind of confidence that Isaiah was trying to convey to the remnant of Israel in the expatriate community in Babylon. Through this promise God was giving a firm guarantee of his love and that he would be watching over the future of the nation at a turning point in history. It was because he was about to create a milestone in history with the overthrow of the Chaldean Empire and the release of the remnant of Israel from slavery to return to their land that he had to give this important promise. His intention was to assure the nation that he was firmly in control of their destiny at this stage before the dawn of the Messianic Era of which the prophet Isaiah was the herald.

This is the promise he gave:

"Though the mountains be shaken and the hills be removed, yet my unfailing love for you will not be shaken nor my covenant of peace be removed, says the Lord, who has compassion on you. O afflicted city, lashed by storms and not comforted, I will build you with stones of turquoise, your foundations with sapphires.
I will make your battlements of rubies, your gates of sparkling jewels, and all your walls of precious stones. All your sons will be taught by the Lord and great will be your children's peace. In righteousness you will be established." Isaiah 54.10 - 14

Revealing the Nature of God

There are some words in Scripture that are outstanding for their beauty and others for their depth of spiritual insight. These words from Isaiah 54 are among the most beautiful and important in the whole of the Bible. They mark a watershed in revelation of the nature of God. They offer a promise that could not be given more firmly or with greater guarantees. It is a promise of God's unfailing love that will remain for ever and ever.

It is a promise of the God of Creation who says that only if the whole created order of the physical universe is dismantled will his love for his people be removed. You cannot get any more cast-iron guarantee than this! It is the kind of dream guarantee that every business corporation embarking on a new venture would love to have. In the world of finance the task of the bankers is to assess the strength of the asset before they will advance a capital loan to support a project.

Here was God giving this incredible promise with the greatest possible guarantee, yet the exiles in Babylon were so stressed by the years of slavery that they were in no way able to receive the promises Isaiah brought to them. Their faith had grown so dull that they could not believe that God cared for them or that he had the power to deliver them. This was why the first messages brought by the prophet in the final years of the exile were all designed to build up confidence in the omnipotent power of Almighty God.

It was only after Isaiah had given the message of Chapters 40 - 44 that he could begin to bring the promise of release from slavery. These five chapters come to a climax in the last verse of

Chapter 44 – the declaration about Cyrus; *'He is my shepherd and will accomplish all that I please; he will say of Jerusalem, "Let it be rebuilt," and of the temple, "Let its foundations be laid".*

Isaiah 44.28

Turning Point in History

Isaiah had to work hard to build up the faith of the downtrodden remnant of Israel and this promise of the unfailing love of God in Chapter 54 is a turning point in the spiritual journey of the nation.

It was a turning point in the history of the world and they were to be the people of promise who would prepare the way for the coming of Messiah. This was what Jeremiah had referred to in the letter he had written to the exiles when he spoke of *'a hope and a future'*. He was foreshadowing the fulfilment of the 'New Covenant' that he had prophesied which God would establish with the house of Israel in preparation for the coming Messiah – the New Covenant would be ratified and fully established through the ministry of Messiah.

The similarity between the words of this promise given to Isaiah and the word given to Jeremiah is quite striking. Jeremiah had said, *"This is what the Lord says, he who appoints the sun to shine by day, who decrees the moon and stars to shine by night, who stirs up the sea so that its waves roar - the Lord Almighty is his name: only if these decrees vanish from my sight, declares the Lord, will the descendants of Israel ever cease to be a nation before me".*

Jeremiah 31.35 - 36

Clearly both prophets had been receiving their guidance from the same source - from the Lord God Almighty, Creator of heaven and earth.

This promise of God's enduring and unbreakable love is the prelude to the announcement of a paradigm shift in world history. Something of incredible importance was about to happen that was comparable with the ancient flood in the time of Noah. This was the significance of the previous verse where Isaiah records God saying, *"To me this is like the days of Noah, when I swore that the waters of Noah would never again cover the earth."* Isaiah 54.9 This statement makes a comparison between the days of Noah and the end of the exile in Babylon. This is highly significant in giving us an understanding of the whole of this important passage in Isaiah 54.

Covenant

The covenant with Noah, at the end of the flood, was a covenant with the whole of mankind. It was not like the covenant with Abraham, or that with Jacob, which were specifically with Israel. At the end of the flood, God said to Noah that the covenant he was making was to be between himself and Noah and 'every living creature'. It was to be a 'covenant for all generations to come' [2]. God promised that there would never again be a flood to destroy the Earth[3] but, *"as long as the Earth endures, seed-time and harvest, cold and heat, summer and winter, day and night, will never cease"* Genesis 8.22. This was a promise of blessing for the benefit of the whole of humanity. It was a turning point in human history, a major milestone.

In the same way, the end of the exile was seen by God to represent a turning point in history, it was, of course, a major event in the history of Israel, but in likening it to 'the days of Noah' God was putting it into a wider perspective. The significance was that the people of Israel were to go back to the land as 'a redeemed people' whom God was preparing to use in the run-up to the Messianic Age where the people of the Old Covenant would become the people of the New Covenant and would be used by God as 'a light for the Gentiles' to take the message of salvation to all nations.

Unfailing Love

The God of Creation who formed the universe and held the destiny of nations in his hands had given a solemn promise that his unfailing love, *hesed*, (the same word that is used in verse eight where it is translated "everlasting kindness") would never be withdrawn: his covenant of peace would never be removed from over the nation. This meant that his 'shalom' that guaranteed health, prosperity and the well-being of the nation would always be with them.

This, of course, was on the understanding that as a redeemed people they would remain faithful to the Lord and be the people whom God could use to prepare the way for Messiah and be a light for the Gentiles to enable him to fulfil his purposes for all people to be able to enter into a personal relationship with him.

---

[2] See Genesis 9.12

[3] See Genesis 9.15

This firm promise of God's unbreakable love being with them throughout the future was sealed with the phrase, *"says the Lord, who has compassion on you"* Isaiah 54.10. It was this phrase that, no doubt, Isaiah hoped would lock the promise into the hearts of the people for ever. Although they were still slaves in an alien land, God had heard their cries and had responded with compassion. This was his promise that whatever happened in the future, his unfailing love would never be removed from them. They would see world-shaking events as Babylon was overthrown and her gods humiliated, but God's love for his people would remain forever. The promise was not only intended for the generation of exiles in Babylon but for their descendants who would repossess the land and restore Jerusalem. They too would see world-shattering events as further empires rose and fell, but God's promise of his abiding love would stand for ever.

Jerusalem

The prophecy then moved from the personal relationship between God and his people to the condition of the City of Jerusalem. It is here that we see further amazing revelations of the nature of God. His tender heart and amazing love is seen in the cry, *"O afflicted city, lashed by storms and not comforted"* Isaiah 54.11. You can be sure that Jesus knew these words. He was familiar with the prophecies of Isaiah. He was given the scroll of Isaiah to read when he entered the synagogue of his hometown in Nazareth [4]. He unrolled the scroll just beyond these words in Chapter 54 and read from Chapter 61, *"The Spirit of the Sovereign Lord is on me because the Lord has anointed me to preach good news to the poor..."*

Sometime later he grieved over the City of Jerusalem, *"O Jerusalem, Jerusalem, you who kill the prophets and stone those sent to you, how often I have longed to gather your children together, as a hen gathers her chicks under her wings, but you were not willing!"* Luke 13.34. Then, in the final week of his earthly ministry as he descended the Mount of Olives overlooking the City, he wept, reflecting the same grief in the heart of the Father that Isaiah had seen and heard more than five centuries earlier. *"If you, even you, had only known on this day what would bring you peace - but now it is hidden from your eyes".*   Luke 19.42

---

[4] See Luke 4.17

Jesus was foreseeing the destruction that the Roman soldiers would carry out not long after his crucifixion and resurrection. Isaiah was expressing God's grief over what the Babylonian soldiers had done to the City in Jeremiah's lifetime. The brief account recorded in Jeremiah Chapter 52 is almost too painful to read as the soldiers ran wild among the helpless civilians when the City defences finally fell after a long siege.

The brutal conquest, as young and old were butchered and raped, houses were ransacked and looted, is a first-hand description that is still shocking even 2,500 years later. The soldiers then forced the people to take part in the destruction of their own beloved City, tearing down the great houses, the palace and even the temple, the great walls and the City gates.

Jerusalem remained in that condition on top of the hill of a much used trade route for everyone to see the humiliation of the proud City of David, of Solomon, of Jehoshaphat and Hezekiah. Reports of the condition of Jerusalem reached the Jewish community in Babylon from travellers which increased the suffering of those who had earlier been taken into slavery. This is vividly portrayed in their community lamentations, *"How deserted lies the city once so full of people!... Bitterly she weeps at night, tears are upon her cheeks... All her gateways are desolate... All the splendour has departed from the daughter of Zion... All who honoured her despise her for they have seen her nakedness".* Lamentations 1.1-8

The humiliation of the once beautiful City of Jerusalem remained for all to see for many years. Jeremiah had prophesied that the destruction of the City would last for 70 years. It was, in fact, 70 years from the destruction of the Temple in 586 BC to the time of its rebuilding in 516 BC recorded by both Haggai and Zephaniah. Before the rebuilding could begin the people had to return from Babylon which could not begin until after the fall of the Babylonian Empire to Cyrus in 539 BC. At the time Isaiah gave this prophecy the City was still in ruins, but he does more than just foretell the rebuilding, he describes what he has heard in his times of intercession with God. God's great love for his people is expressed in his compassion for the City he loved.

New Jerusalem

The thing that is so amazing in the words that Isaiah brought was that God's intention was not simply to rebuild it as it had been.

It was not just a restoration that he planned, but this was to be a New Jerusalem - the City of God that would be so splendid it would be as if all its buildings were overlaid with precious stones that sparkled in the sunshine and radiated its beauty. Travellers would be able to see the light of the sun reflected from its walls from many miles distant. It was this description that came with a special message to the people still enslaved in Babylon saying that God's intention was far more than a mere restoration of ancient ruins. His intention was to create something new that would be a thing of beauty for all the world to behold. It would be a City with its foundations built of precious stones. The design, construction and the final completion would be carried out by none other than God himself as Architect and Builder of the New Jerusalem.[5]

This description of the New Jerusalem was intended to convey a deep spiritual message to the people in slavery whom God was about to redeem. They were to be the firstborn people of a New Covenant among whom the presence of God would dwell forever. It was, of course, a picture of salvation and a message to a dispirited, shattered and poverty-stricken people of what God can do to transform the lives of those who trust him. They would see the work of salvation of their God reclaiming his people from bondage and restoring them to the city of promise. For each of those who received this message it was a promise of new life out of the depths of despair.

Changed Lives

In our pastoral ministry in some of the toughest areas of London, Monica and I have seen many people whose lives have been dramatically changed through an encounter with Jesus. Even hardened criminals, or young men with a string of convictions, can change when they are faced, not with a God of judgement, but with the love of a Saviour who has good plans for them and actually gives the power to change. They already have plenty of experience of judgement from the world, but it is the experience of love that softens them and leads to transformation. One of the many transformed lives we saw was a young man who was a gang leader in the East End of London. When he came to faith he immediately threw himself enthusiastically into doing good

---

[5] See Hebrews 11.10 and Revelation 2.1

works. He joined our little team of volunteers who were converting a shop into a play-group-centre for local mums and toddlers.

Late one evening the team ran out of timber for constructing shelves. He immediately volunteered to help saying that there was a timber yard nearby and he would go and get some. The team leader reminded him that it was night time, and the yard would be closed. "Yes, of course, I know that!" He retorted, in a slightly scornful note, as he disappeared out into the dark. On his return, flushed with success, the team leader had the moral dilemma of what to do. He wisely delayed a confrontation, thanking him for the timber and saying that he would visit the yard himself in the morning and speak to the owners.

This kind of dilemma was not unusual as moral values linked with the local culture do not change rapidly in response to a spiritual experience. On one occasion we were redecorating and refurbishing a church hall with lots of local volunteer help. Everyone was keen to have a share in the action by bringing food for the workers or gifts of paint or other materials for the work. One man came and presented Monica with a box of electric light bulbs saying that he had noticed that a number of bulbs needed replacing. She thanked him for his generous gift and said that they would be useful not just in the Hall but in other parts of the premises. It was several days later that a member of staff pointed out to her that each of the light bulbs was stamped with the words "London Borough of Newham" – another moral dilemma!

Each of these situations required careful and sensitive handling to ensure that new found faith was not burned up on the altar of moral righteousness, but in virtually every case we found that love and patience found a way. The gang leader who responded to the love of Jesus in his own life became a strong advocate for the faith and led most of his erstwhile followers to know the Lord.

Paul's statement that *"If anyone is in Christ, he is a new creation; the old has gone, the new has come"* 2 Corinthians 5.17 was certainly true in his life. His whole lifestyle changed to meet the new objectives. Everyone who knew him could see the change and most of his family and friends were amazed. At first they scoffed and said it wouldn't last – he'd be back to normal soon, but as the weeks went by they got more and more curious and wanted to know what had happened to him, which gave him the opportunity for some serious conversations. His friends had to make a choice; either they dropped him or they followed his lead. For many of them his personal witness was compelling.

Creative Action

The picture of the 'New Jerusalem' in Isaiah 54 represents not simply the physical rebuilding of the city but a dramatic spiritual change in the covenant people of God. The change would be the result of God making his dwelling in the City. It was a pictorial statement of God's intention to give new life to people who had been broken by bondage and would now be living lives of radiant beauty reflecting the glory of the Lord.

For the people in Babylon who thought that God had abandoned them it was an amazing discovery to find that God had not only been grieving, but had actually entered into their suffering as he identified with the crumbling ruins of the City that bore his name. This identification did not simply end in extending sympathy - it brought action - creative action - transforming the old Jerusalem and bringing forth the New Jerusalem in the same way as God transforms the lives of those who respond to his love.

The final statement in this passage not only sealed that promise of new life but also gave the key to understanding the way in which the new creation of transformed lives and transformed communities and transformed cities would be accomplished. *"All your sons will be taught by the Lord, and great will be your children's peace"* Isaiah 54.13. That key lies in 'personal relationships' and this was at the heart of the great truth about God revealed through the prophets.

The prophets perceived that the God of Abraham, Isaac and Jacob - the God of their forefathers - was not like the gods of the other nations, created out of bits of wood and stone, inanimate objects. He was actually the Creator of the Universe and although he was unseen he could be known, through observing his works in creation, through observing his activity in the world and among the nations, and through listening to him. It was this last attribute of God that was of primary significance to the prophets who learned to recognise when God was speaking to them, to understand what he was saying, and to interpret it to the people.

Taught by the Lord

In this prophecy of Isaiah, *"all your sons will be taught by the Lord"* that ability to listen to God was being extended to all people. Through the prophet, God was promising that the day would come when he would fulfil the promise he had given to Jeremiah of a 'New Covenant' with his people - a new relationship that would enable each one to communicate with God in a personal way. Each one would be able to hear directly from God and not have to rely upon priests or other holy men to interpret God's word to them.

It's rather like reading a book by some famous teacher whom you really admire and you greatly benefit from his teaching. Then you have the opportunity of listening to a CD of the man giving an important lecture and you understand the teaching much more clearly than just having read the book. Then you hear that this famous teacher is going to give a lecture in a nearby town. You resolve to go to hear him. It is a life changing experience. The teaching you had first read in the book now comes alive for you in a new way because you have heard it from the mouth of the man himself.

But suppose someone takes you backstage after the lecture, someone who is a friend of the teacher, and introduces you, so that you have the opportunity of talking personally with him. Now his teaching takes on a new dimension in your life because you know the teacher personally. When you next read his book it is as though you can actually hear him speaking the words. You can even hear the intonation in his voice. His words come alive for you in a new way.

This is what happens when we are introduced to Jesus. Because he is the *'Word made flesh'*, the presence of God in human form, we are able to have a personal relationship with God which brings alive the teaching that he first gave to the Patriarchs and to his servant Moses. The remarkable thing is that the Prophets discovered this personal relationship with God hundreds of years before the coming of Messiah Jesus.

God actually called Abraham his 'friend'. Isaiah reminded the people who were in slavery in Babylon of this when he was bringing them the good news that God was about to release them from bondage and take them back to Jerusalem.

He reminded them of their heritage in some unforgettable words,

"But you, O Israel, my servant, Jacob, whom I have chosen, you descendants of Abraham my friend, I took you from the ends of the earth, from its farthest corners I called you. I said, 'you are my servant; I have chosen you and have not rejected you. So do not fear, for I am with you; do not be dismayed, for I am your God. I will strengthen you and help you; I will uphold you with my righteous right hand'". Isaiah 41.8 - 10

Friends

In a highly significant conversation with his disciples Jesus defined the personal relationship he had established with them. He told his disciples that they were his friends if they did what he commanded them; loving him and each other. This is an incredible statement showing the level of divine revelation available to those who accept Jesus as their personal Lord and Saviour and enter into this new relationship with God through him. The truth about God is no longer solely drawn from the words we read in the books of the Bible, but they come alive for us through the activity of the Holy Spirit as an outcome of the special relationship into which we are privileged to enter through Jesus.

Isaiah was foreseeing the work of the Messiah in establishing this new relationship which Jesus was later to call the 'Kingdom of God'. In the revelation given to Isaiah it was the 'New Jerusalem' that would have the presence of God as a living reality within the City so that all the residents would be aware of God's presence in a highly personal manner, which would not only transform their own relationship with God but would transform their relationships with other human beings.

This is the measure of the remarkable depth of revelation given to the great prophets of Israel who first learned to enter the presence of God and to dwell in the City of God long before the physical rebuilding of the City and hundreds of years before the coming of Messiah who laid the spiritual foundations of the New Jerusalem. They were already dwellers in the new City whose Architect and Builder was the Lord God Almighty.

Chapter Six

GOD'S LOVE SONG

This chapter looks at the message underlying Isaiah of Jerusalem's 'Song of the Vineyard' which reveals God's grief at the unresponsiveness of his people and his unfailing love offered to them under all circumstances. It ends with the promise that God will actually sing to us!

The Song of the Vineyard

The first seven verses of Isaiah 5 are known as 'The Song of the Vineyard'. It is one of the prophetic masterpieces of the Old Testament and is not only a song but also a parable. In these verses Isaiah of Jerusalem uses an unusual method of communicating his message, which contrasts the grapes of wrath, with a tale of God's mercy.

The first two verses describe the 'plot' of the parable:

'I will sing for the one I love a song about his vineyard.

My loved one had a vineyard on a fertile hillside.

He dug it up and cleared it of stones and planted it with the choicest vines.

He built a watchtower in it and cut out a winepress as well,

Then he looked for a crop of good grapes, but it yielded only bad fruit.'

Background

In order to understand the impact of this song a little background is required. It comes from the early part of Isaiah of Jerusalem's ministry in the Eighth Century BC when there was mounting opposition to the prophet's words. He had been bringing some very strong warnings about idolatry and unfaithfulness to God.

The people saw nothing wrong with joining in the festivals of the local Canaanite cults as well as worshipping the God of their fathers. They were happy to accept local beliefs and customs as they thought it was necessary to pay homage to the local gods who controlled the weather and the fertility of the land.

The sex cults of the Canaanites, that involved sympathetic magic to induce greater fertility from the land in order to produce better crops, had been popular with the Hebrew tribes (especially the men!) since their settlement in the land. Isaiah of Jerusalem protested strongly against these idolatrous practices which he said were breaking the covenant relationship with the God of their fathers: Abraham, Isaac and Jacob. He was particularly savage in his condemnation of the religious practices of the Hebrew priests who taught that so long as the people offered the right animal sacrifices as laid down by Moses they could do whatever they liked. He called them *"A sinful nation, a people loaded with guilt, a brood of evildoers, children given to corruption!"* Isaiah 1.4 - not exactly diplomatic language!

Unpopular Message

It is small wonder that the prophet was not popular with the political leaders, or the people. But he went even farther in alienating the priests with declarations such as, *"The multitude of your sacrifices - what are they to me? says the Lord. I have had more than enough of burnt offerings, of the fat of fattened animals; I have no pleasure in the blood of bulls and lambs and goats... stop bringing meaningless offerings!"* Isaiah 1.11

He further alienated not only the priests but all the people by telling them that God would not listen to their prayers. *"When you spread out your hands in prayer, I will hide my eyes from you; even if you offer many prayers, I will not listen. Your hands are full of blood; wash and make yourselves clean. Take your evil deeds out of my sight! Stop doing wrong, learn to do right! Seek justice, encourage the oppressed. Defend the cause of the fatherless, plead the case of the widow."* Isaiah 1.15 - 17

New Prophetic Strategy

It is no great surprise to learn that Isaiah of Jerusalem was not universally popular and had few friends in the capital city. Here he attempts an entirely new strategy. He probably stood up on a raised pillar in the middle of a busy street-market in the heart of the City of Jerusalem and announced his new song, accompanying himself on some kind of stringed instrument.

The sight of this much-derided prophet was guaranteed to excite the people and many came running to see what would happen to him this time and whether he would be arrested or pelted with rotting fruit. Certainly the prophet had no difficulty in gathering a crowd! But this was probably the first time he had ever sung to them! They were more used to hearing him shouting condemnatory messages. He began playing and singing quite softly at first.

Curious Crowd

As the song developed the crowd grew in number and those in the front shuffled closer as others pressed in behind, trying to catch the words. Some of them would have been peasant farmers who had come into Jerusalem for market day. They were used to tending the land and would have had no difficulty in understanding the description of work in a vineyard.

All the people in the crowd would have been familiar with the kind of scene described. It was a picture of a fertile hillside cleared of large stones, which the gardener used to form a wall around the vineyard. He dug the soil and prepared it carefully, and then he planted the best vines obtainable in Israel. He dug out a wine vat in the rocky ground where the grapes were to be trodden and the juice would run along channels into the storage containers.

Everything was done to ensure a good harvest and to protect the crop from vandals and robbers. But when the time came for the vines to produce their crop only small, hard, sour grapes appeared that set the teeth on edge and were completely useless. They were no use either to eat or to make into wine. This was something that everyone in the crowd, and especially the farmers, could understand and they would have had some sympathy with the gardener.

A Rap Song

At this point the song took a new twist as the prophetic singer now appealed directly to his hearers.

'Now you dwellers in Jerusalem and men of Judah judge between me and my vineyard. What more could have been done for my vineyard than I have done for it?

When I looked for good grapes, why did it yield only bad?'

The form and cadence of this lyric indicates that the prophet was using a novel kind of song similar to what would today be known as 'Rap'. By this time he had, no doubt, attracted a large crowd and both the music and words were gripping the attention of the people.

The prophet was appealing to the sympathy of his hearers. He wanted them to act as witnesses that the gardener had done everything possible to ensure that good fruit came from his vineyard. He had cleared the ground of all the stones and large bits of rock. He had carefully tended the soil and had dug in rich compost. He had sought the choicest vines in the market and carefully planted them with supporting stakes to give them security and strength against strong winds and storms. He had regularly watered them ensuring that their roots never ran dry. Then he expected to be able to harvest a good crop of fine grapes.

Crowd Involvement

The people in the crowd were then invited to act as judge between the gardener and his vineyard in the same way that God had once used the prophet Nathan to accuse King David concerning his adultery with Bathsheba, his beautiful next-door neighbour. Nathan had told a story in which he had persuaded David to act as judge before the king had realised that he was, in fact, acting as his own judge in the matter of his adultery with his neighbour's wife [1].

Isaiah's song began to move into the point where the people were fully involved in the story. At this stage of the parable the audience still did not realise that they were being set up to act as judge and jury in their own case. God's complaint against his people was that he had surrounded them with loving kindness and had lavished upon them every kind of blessing and yet they had spurned his love, turning away from the paths of righteousness into sin. So God cried out to his people, 'What more could I have done for you than I have already done?'

Stunned Silence

Suddenly the melody became more strident and the people stood in stunned silence as the prophetic song declared the verdict,

---

[1] See 2 Samuel 12

'Now I will tell you what I am going to do to my vineyard: I will take away its hedge, and it will be destroyed; I will break down its wall, and it will be trampled.'

Isaiah 5.5

The audience must have been growing uncomfortably aware that this was no ordinary song. It slowly dawned upon them that they were being involved in a drama of far greater significance than the mere failure of a grape harvest. It was the gardener himself, as owner of the vineyard, who pronounced judgment, *'I will tell you what I am going to do with my vineyard.'*

The vineyard over which the gardener had lavished care and protection would see its hedge removed, exposing it to strong winds which would blow away the blossom, the first signs of fruit. The wall would be broken down, leaving it exposed to the attacks of wild animals and robbers. The cultivated land would be neglected, the weeds would not be removed nor the branches pruned. Drought would starve the plants of water. Wild thorns and thistles would grow on the land and choke the vines.

Prophetic Purpose Achieved

By this time the people listening to the song must have perceived that the parable was directed against them. The uncultivated land was a familiar sight in areas plundered by an enemy. The threat implied in the parable was inescapable. The song was beginning to achieve its prophetic purpose.

Suddenly there was no doubt. The owner of the vineyard was none other than the Lord God Almighty, for he alone had the ability to say, *'I will command the clouds not to rain upon it.'* The audience could do no more than wait sullenly for the final pronouncement, *'The vineyard of the Lord Almighty is the house of Israel, and the men of Judah are the garden of his delight.'*

Isaiah 5.7

Israel and Judah had broken their covenant relationship with God. They had freely entered into solemn promises of faithfulness to the Lord and to be obedient to his word, but they had subsequently been unfaithful to him and turned away. *'He looked for justice, but saw bloodshed; for righteousness, but heard cries of distress.'*

Isaiah 5.7

The people were too shocked and stunned even to pick up stones to throw at the prophet. One by one they hung their heads and turned away in sullen defiance. They knew that what he had said was true but they were too full of guilty anger even to protest. They hated what they had heard and they especially resented having been tricked into listening to the message of this wily prophet who always managed to make them feel uncomfortable. The crowd rapidly dispersed leaving Isaiah of Jerusalem with just his tiny band of faithful supporters and eager young disciples. They were all left wondering, would the message make any difference? Clearly it had made an impact but had the seriousness of the challenge really been understood?

Would there be Repentance?

Would there be any change in the behaviour of the people? Would the priests and political rulers realise the heinous offence they were giving to God by their idolatry and their deliberate breaking of the covenant relationship that had, for so many years, been the guarantee of safety and prosperity of the nation? Would there be repentance and turning in the nation, which was the only thing that could guarantee the protection of Judah in the face of the onslaught of the Assyrian Empire? The situation on the international front was so serious that it was quite literally true that only a full-scale spiritual revival could save the nation from destruction. The power of the Assyrian army was such that the defences of Judah would be unable to withstand the assault. Only divine intervention could save the nation and God would not protect an unholy, unrighteous and unfaithful people who had deliberately broken their covenant relationship with him.

Relevance for Today

This message has great relevance for us today. God is infinitely patient and his love and mercy endure forever. But there comes a point when, because of the free-will he has given to us, God has to let us go along the way we have chosen. He then withdraws his cover of protection. Otherwise he would be denying his own nature of holiness, justice and integrity. Parents of adolescent young people will understand the dilemma in the heart of God as he grieves over his wayward children having done all he could to warn them and protect them as loving parents do for their children. Many Christian parents go through times of great anxiety and suffering as their children grow up and begin to exercise their independence. They feel helpless when they see their children, like the prodigal son, 'going into the far country' and getting their lives into a mess. Like the gardener in the song of the vineyard, they ask, 'What more could I have done?'

God's Unbreakable Love

But just as we never cease to love our children, so God never ceases to love us. When his warnings are ignored he appeals to us to return to him by reminding us of his unbreakable love. But when his appeal is ignored he can do no other than remove his protection from his rebellious and unrighteous children.

It is at that point that God stands back from our lives and awaits the moment when, under the impact of hardship or of the enemy's attacks upon us, we cry out to him for help. At that very moment God's love and compassion triumphs over adversity, for we are open to the message of Calvary, and to receiving his forgiveness. Then we are ready to have our sins washed away by his love and to be restored to a right relationship with him whom the Lord Jesus taught us to know as our Father in heaven.

If we can love our children with an unbreakable love, then we need to remember that this is but a pale reflection of God's unceasing love for us. *'What more could I have done for you?'* is still the cry of God's heart to all those who are unfaithful to him; while he says to those who are penitent and who are seeking his love and forgiveness, *"With everlasting kindness I will have compassion on you,....my unfailing love for you will not be shaken"*.

Isaiah 54.8 - 10

The Need for Love

The phrase, *"What more could I have done for you?"* on the lips of human beings can sometimes mean that all the wrong things have been done for our children. There are many parents who lavish material things upon their children but do not give them the very thing that the children most crave - the love and security of the two people who mean most to them. That also means setting boundaries and enforcing rules in the lives of our children that actually give security and enable them to establish standards in their own character development.

Loving parents do not simply cast their children adrift among their peer group at the beginning of their social experience of the world around them. They take note of the friendships made by their children and gently steer them away from harmful influences while encouraging healthy contacts. God does exactly the same with us, his children, if we learn to know his word and listen to him as he speaks to us.

The prophet Isaiah did just that. In Chapter 54.4 he tells us how he learned to listen to God. His secret was to use the early hours of the morning. He says, *"The Sovereign Lord has given me an instructed tongue, to know the word that sustains the weary. He wakens me morning by morning, wakens my ear to listen like one being taught. The Sovereign Lord has opened my ears."* He says that in the same way as a student metaphorically sits at the feet of his favourite professor and listens attentively in order not to miss a single word, so he had learned to listen attentively to God. His relationship was so close that the Spirit of God awoke him each morning with an awareness of his presence.

Learning to Listen

I myself have learned to use the precious early morning hours and to allow the Spirit of God to wake me each morning with his presence. I lie very still, listening to him, seeking to know if there is anything that he has been communicating to me during the night, or if there is something special that is going to happen during the day to which he wants to draw my attention. Those early morning hours are of great importance in my spiritual life. Before ever I have any human conversation I come into the presence of God and seek to know what he is saying to me. This sets the tone for the day and ensures that I begin with the right focus and in the confidence that I am in the centre of the will of the Lord for my life.

Often in my early morning quiet times I think of the great prophet Isaiah who had trained his body to awake before the sunlight spread across the sky and had learned to recognise the voice of the Lord as he listened silently. I think of how privileged I am to know that the Lord Jesus is my advocate at the throne of grace and that through him I not only have access to the Father but I have his unique revelation of the nature and purposes of God.

The writing prophets of Israel such as Isaiah, Jeremiah and Ezekiel, had none of the rich teaching of the New Testament to guide them. They did, of course, have Moses and the record of the ministries of men such as Samuel, Elijah and Elisha, but a great deal of the messages they declared to the nation had to come through direct revelation from God. Isaiah likened himself to a student, *"one being taught"* and this is exactly how the prophets conducted their ministries – learning all the time more about God and sharing it with their disciples and declaring it publicly to the people or taking messages privately to the rulers of the nation.

Change of Ministry

One of the most difficult periods in my own ministry was when God called us to leave pastoring a large and prosperous church in North London and take a rundown church in the East End of London with a tiny congregation where Monica and I could develop some new concepts in community-based evangelism without being hindered by tradition. Our new pastorate could not afford to support us but we knew that God had told us to go there so we had to find another way of supporting our young family. I was fortunate enough to secure a senior lectureship in London University teaching the Sociology of Religion, and Monica taught evening classes in adult education while I babysat.

Although I was academically well qualified I had never done any teaching in my life – only preaching, which is quite a different style. It was an entirely new experience and the first two years were a nightmare. Every lecture had to be prepared fresh. I had nothing to fall back on; no previous lecture notes to use. In addition, I had to maintain my church work and preach on Sundays and we had three children, one of whom was still a baby.

I knew exactly what Isaiah meant when he said *"The Sovereign Lord has given me an instructed tongue, to know the word that sustains the weary."* I would not only go to bed weary but most mornings I would wake weary! Maybe Isaiah also had to cope with a crying baby in the night. We know that he was a family man as we have a record of some of the strange names he gave his children.[2] But more importantly he had to learn to be a prophet and throughout his life he knew himself to be a student as well as a minister of the word of God.

---

[2] See Isaiah 7.3 and 8.3

Learning and Teaching

I had the same experience. I was a 'student' as well as a teacher. Day by day (and often night by night!) I would be poring through textbooks and study papers as well as my own research-findings to prepare the next day's lecture for my students. The great prophets of Israel such as Isaiah and Jeremiah had to do their own research and although, very possibly, they had access to the books of Moses and the record of the kings of Israel, they were pioneers in receiving revelation of the nature and purposes of God. What was probably even more demanding was that they lived in incredibly difficult times of international turmoil when great empires were clashing and threatening to annihilate smaller nations like Lebanon, Edom, Moab, Israel and Judah. At the same time the Hebrew nation itself was being shaken by social change, moral uncertainty and spiritual apostasy.

God's timing is always perfect and each of the prophets of Israel and Judah arrived on the scene at a time of crisis – international as well as national. Although each had a distinctive mission there was a pattern to their ministry that involved reminding the nation of their history; highlighting the deeds of the Lord - the things that he had done for his people in the past - and, most importantly, bringing a direct word from the Lord concerning the present situation. This served to remind them of the covenant established with God through their forefathers and the faithfulness as well as the almighty power of God.

Progressive Revelation

Each of the prophets was also a teacher charged with responsibility for informing the nation about the requirements of the Lord. This also involved a type of 'progressive revelation' of the very nature of God through which the prophets not only emphasised earlier teaching but also added to the body of 'received knowledge' an understanding of God that was newly revealed to enable them to deal with the contemporary situation each of them had to face. It is through this additional revelation of the nature and purposes of God that we have benefited from their writings; all of which, of course, prepared the way for the full and final revelation of the Father through the Lord Jesus our Saviour.

In this prophetic song in Isaiah Chapter 5 the final verse of the song gives what was probably new revelation to many of the people listening to the prophet in 8th-century Jerusalem. Of all the great prophets of Israel in this period only Amos and Hosea had preceded Isaiah of Jerusalem and their ministries and mission were in the northern kingdom based in Samaria. Micah was a contemporary, although somewhat younger than Isaiah of Jerusalem, and he lived in a provincial town and was not so familiar with the great city of Jerusalem, neither did he have the breadth of international knowledge of the older man.

Isaiah of Jerusalem had an intimate knowledge of life in the City He gives a vivid description of the pride and affluence of women walking the streets *"tripping along with mincing steps, with ornaments jingling on their ankles"* Isaiah 3.16. His description of the judgement that was about to fall upon Jerusalem[3] must have created terror in the hearts of all the people and the final verse of his song gave the reason why God would allow such a calamity to befall the people of the City that symbolised his presence.

"The vineyard of the Lord Almighty is the house of Israel, and the men of Judah are the garden of his delight. And he looked for justice, but saw bloodshed; for righteousness, but heard cries of distress" Isaiah 5.7. Judah was really precious to God. He had lavished his care upon the people, doing everything possible to provide for their welfare and happiness. The land was incredibly fertile, producing all the food needed for the population and the City was well provided with water and natural defences.

All the people had to do was to live peacefully with one another, maintaining good relationships and living lives of honesty, integrity and justice in all their dealings with each other; guarding moral values in business and in family life and marriage. In their spiritual lives they had to avoid getting involved in the religious practices of other people and only worship the God and Father of Abraham, Isaac and Jacob - having no other God than him.

Apostasy

Sadly, they not only joined in the religious practices and festivals of the Canaanites and other groups who had shrines on the high places in the land, but they also were unjust and quarrelsome in their relationships with one another and got into all sorts of sexually immoral practices that resulted in marriage and family

---

[3] See Isaiah 3.1 - 15

breakdown. Isaiah of Jerusalem's long ministry that spanned four kings of Judah began with strong warnings of judgement and predictions of disaster but saw an event of amazing deliverance towards the end of his life when he joined King Hezekiah in intercession to repel the Assyrian invasion. Sennacherib's army suffered a sudden catastrophe losing 185,000 men overnight which forced him to lift the siege of Jerusalem and withdraw [4].

The Song in Chapter 5, however, comes from the earlier part of his ministry, possibly during the reign of King Ahaz [5] who was one of the most godless men to occupy the throne of Judah. He actually encouraged people to worship other gods. He closed the temple, barred the doors and *"set up altars at every street corner in Jerusalem"*.[6] Isaiah's pronouncements of judgement upon the leaders of the nation thundered through the streets of the City, *"The Lord Almighty has a day in store for all the proud and lofty... the arrogance of man will be brought low and the pride of men humbled... men will flee to caves in the rocks and to holes in the ground from the dread of the Lord and the splendour of his Majesty, when he rises to shake the earth".*   Isaiah 2.12 - 19

God's Grief

This straight confrontational tactic clearly hadn't worked; there was no national repentance, so in his song the prophet tried to get the people to see something of the heart of God. He appealed to their sense of justice and tried to get them to see how they would feel if they had done everything possible to provide for the welfare of people whom they loved, and then they were spurned. The people of Israel were God's delight whom he had surrounded with his love, expecting them to live together in harmony, but instead everywhere he looked there was violence and bloodshed.

Instead of there being right relationships, they were oppressing one another and causing cries of distress. Consequently, God was grieving over his people; not simply with the distressed but he was also grieving over the whole nation that had turned their

---

[4] See Isaiah 37.36

[5] Isaiah's call to ministry 'in the year that King Uzziah died' (Isaiah 6.1) was in 744 BC. Following Jotham's short reign, Ahaz came to the throne in 741 BC so the date for this song is probably around 740 – 735 BC.

[6] See 2 Chronicles 28. 24

backs upon him and was thereby putting them outside his loving protection and causing the whole nation to be vulnerable to the attacks of outside enemies.

Isaiah was not the first to put this kind of message into a song. Similar sentiments are found in many of the Psalms - the Song Book of Israel. Psalm 81, which probably comes from the same period as Isaiah of Jerusalem's song, has these words, *"Hear, O my people and I will warn you - if you would but listen to me O Israel! You shall have no other god among you; you shall not bow down to an alien god. I am the Lord your God who brought you up out of Egypt. Open wide your mouth and I will fill it. But my people would not listen to me; Israel would not submit to me. So I gave them over to their stubborn hearts to follow their own devices. If my people would listen to me, if Israel would follow my ways, how quickly would I subdue their enemies... you would be fed with the finest of wheat; with honey from the rock I would satisfy you."*
Psalm 81.8 - 16

These words reflect the grief in God's heart that the prophet was trying to convey to the nation in his song. The warnings of judgement were mixed with pleading for the nation to recognise the danger that was facing them as a direct consequence of their idolatry, which put them outside the protection of the God of their fathers. Yet he continued to love them because he was a covenant-keeping God who had given his promise to their forefathers. If only the people would listen to him he would not only protect them from their enemies but he would lavish upon them rich food in the land of milk and honey that he had given to them.

God's Unfailing Love

This theme of God's goodness to his people and his everlasting love is expressed time after time in the poetic songs of Israel from the earliest pre-exilic Psalms to those that clearly come from a post-exilic period; right down to about 100 BC when the Book of Psalms is known to have been in its present form. The phrase *"your unfailing love"* occurs no less than 25 times from Psalm 6 to Psalm 147. This is not to suggest that the Psalms are in any kind of chronological order, but simply to note that in every period of the history of Israel the 'unfailing love of God' was recognised and was continually in the words sung by the people.

There is an interesting reference in the words of one of Jeremiah's contemporaries, Zephaniah, which reflects similar thoughts to those expressed in Isaiah's song a century earlier. It is found in Zephaniah 3.14-17 where the prophet was urging people to sing and shout aloud: to be glad and rejoice because he was foreseeing a time coming when God would forgive his people and once again surround them with his love and protection. It was written during the reign of Josiah in the very early part of Jeremiah's ministry, which was a time of considerable prosperity. Josiah had instituted a moral and spiritual reform. He had renewed the covenant with the Lord following the discovery of what is thought to be the Book of Deuteronomy during repairs to the temple. He had torn down all the detestable idols installed by Manasseh, his father, and called for a nationwide celebration of Passover with great celebrations in Jerusalem.

Zephaniah seems to have had a great deal more confidence in Josiah's Reform than the far-seeing Jeremiah that this was a significant spiritual turning point in the nation, so he called for this time of rejoicing. Jeremiah, although approving of King Josiah, was more sceptical that the Reform would lead to national spiritual revival.[7]

God Quietens our Fears

No doubt God was pleased with the leadership that King Josiah showed and the response of the people in turning away from their idolatrous practices. Zephaniah wanted to see the people praising God with unrestrained joy. He said *"Do not fear, O Zion; do not let your hands hang limp. The Lord your God is with you, he is mighty to save. He will take great delight in you, he will quiet you with his love and will rejoice over you with singing"*. Isaiah 3.16-17 Isaiah of Jerusalem had said that the people of Judah were the garden of God's delight but at this time the nation was being led by a godless king: there was idolatry everywhere and communal chaos - violence and bloodshed, injustice and oppression - the social results of spiritual apostasy. Now, with a God-fearing king on the throne there were signs of social as well as spiritual reform.

There was still plenty of danger on the international front with Egypt and Assyria each seeking to exert dominance over the

---

[7] See Jeremiah 4.10-31

smaller nations and to extend their empires over the region.

So the word of the Lord was one of reassurance that he is mighty to save. When his children put their trust in him this gives him great delight and he puts his covering of protection over the land. The message God gave to Zephaniah was that he was seeking to quieten their fears with his love and that God was rejoicing in the newfound faith of his people after the terrible years of apostasy under Manasseh.

God Sings a Love Song

The prophet Zephaniah saw God acting as a loving parent comforting a fearful child. As a mother sometimes goes to a child in the darkness of the night to comfort the infant after a nightmare, so God was reaching out to his children to comfort them after the nightmare experience of Manasseh's reign. If the child is severely disturbed the mother will lift him out of bed into the comfort of her arms, holding his face close to hers so that he can feel the warmth of her body and draw comfort from that close contact. When the child has been quietened by the mother's love she puts him back into bed but instead of walking away she sits by the bedside and sings to him. This is exactly what Zephaniah says that God does with his children. He quietens them with his love and actually sings to them.

This is the only place in the Bible where God is said to sing to us. There are many places where we are exhorted to sing praises to God, but here the Lord himself actually sings to us to comfort us when we are disturbed and to bring into our lives his peace which passes human understanding. Such is the measure of God's love for us that he stays by our side even after his love has quietened our fears.

This is a prophetic foretaste of the teaching Jesus gave to his disciples saying that he would never leave them comfortless. He would come to them and abide with them. If they obeyed his teaching to love one another they would remain in his love just as he obeyed his Father's command and remained in his love.[8]

Such is the unbreakable love of the Father for us, his children.

---

[8] See John 15.10

GOD'S LOVE CHANGES A NATION

This chapter focuses upon Jeremiah, the man who faithfully brought the word of God to the nation for forty years. It examines his message which showed God's unbreakable love and that God desired to see the reuniting of the divided tribes of Israel and the transformation of the nation.

Message of Warning

The prophet Jeremiah had a most unenviable mission. It was probably the most difficult and unrewarding ministry of all the prophets of ancient Israel. For 40 years he tramped the streets of Jerusalem and other cities in the southern state of Judah declaring a message of warning. His warnings were ignored. He himself was subjected to abuse and social ostracism. He was banned from the temple so he stood outside in the courtyard publicly declaring the word of the Lord. He was put in the stocks and publicly humiliated. He was dropped down a filthy well and left to die but was secretly rescued by one of his supporters.

All this abuse was because the message he was bringing was hated by the authorities - both state and religious. The message was unchanging throughout the years: it was a call for the nation to put their trust in the God of their fathers. The message got him involved in international politics as well as domestic, religious and social issues. It was a day of ambitious leaders of powerful empires vying to control the whole Middle Eastern world. After the decline of Assyria the political leaders in Jerusalem sought an alliance with their old enemies in Egypt against the rising power of Babylon. Jeremiah railed against such stupidity which would inevitably bring the wrath of Nebuchadnezzar and his ruthless army against the cities of Judah.

After a series of weak kings the inevitable happened: the land was invaded, villages and towns were torn apart, the population slaughtered or reduced to slavery. Even the great well-fortified city of Lachish, built by Solomon, had fallen. Only Jerusalem remained defiant. Throughout this time and right up until the siege of Jerusalem began with the Babylonian army surrounding the walls, Jeremiah continued to call for repentance and turning, saying that even at the eleventh hour God would forgive and protect the city and its people if there were genuine repentance and faith in God. With leaders and the people obdurate and the enemy already preparing for a final assault upon the city walls, Jeremiah suddenly changed the message he had been giving for forty years. There was no longer any point in calling for repentance and turning. Judgement was inevitable upon the nation.

Change of Message

Three times he heard the Lord telling him to stop praying for the nation - a devastating command! And now with the enemy siege ramps against the walls of Jerusalem he heard God telling him to declare a remarkable message of love. It was:

'I have loved you with an everlasting love; I have drawn you with loving-kindness. I will build you up again and you will be rebuilt, O Virgin Israel'.   Jeremiah 31.3,4

This was a major change in the message that Jeremiah had been bringing to the nation. It was at this point in his ministry that he introduced the theme of a future change in the nation's fortunes. He said that there would come a time of restoration when God would once again bless the nation. Instead of famine there would be an abundant harvest; instead of economic hardship there would be prosperity, instead of sorrow there would be joy. *'Again you will take up your tambourines and go out to dance with the joyful'.*   Jeremiah 31.4

It is almost impossible to conceive the significance of this message coming as it did with the Babylonian army poised to take the city. Yet it is a measure of the unchanging love of God that he should send such a message at a time when tremendous fear was gripping the entire population. The Babylonian army, noted for its cruelty and the ruthless behaviour of its soldiers, was about to be unleashed upon the people. As Jeremiah had foretold, Egypt had failed to come to Judah's aid, despite their solemn promises. The diplomatic landscape was strewn with broken pacts and treaties. Jeremiah had constantly warned that this would happen and that only trust in God could stave off a national disaster.

Promise of Restoration

As the inevitability of defeat dawned upon the people, Jeremiah changed the message to a declaration of the faithfulness of God; his unchanging love and his firm promises of restoration. With the enemy now at the gates of Jerusalem recriminations and looking back over the past would do no good. The prophet began to look forward beyond the disaster. What he was hearing from God was how he would work out his purposes for the nation despite their unfaithfulness.

Jeremiah must have realised that he was standing at one of the great milestones in history. He had foreseen that, with the nation steeped in idolatry and refusing to put their trust in the God of their fathers, judgment was bound to follow. It was an inevitable consequence of rebellion against God. At the same time he knew that the love and mercy of God would never allow Israel to be totally destroyed. He would find a way of bringing blessing out of disaster, good out of evil and transforming tragedy into triumph.

Although the people would be driven into exile, scattered among the nations, Jeremiah knew that the day would come when God would re-gather them to the land and pour out his blessings upon them because he is a faithful God who keeps his covenant promises forever. Jeremiah also foresaw that God was going to work out his purposes in a most amazing way. So at the end of chapter 30 we find him repeating the words of severe warning that he had used earlier in his ministry[1]. *"See, the storm of the Lord will burst out in wrath, a driving wind swirling down on the heads of the wicked. The fierce anger of the Lord will not turn back until he fully accomplishes the purposes of his heart. In days to come you will understand this."* Jeremiah 30.23 - 24

The End of Israel?

What Jeremiah was perceiving was so utterly revolutionary that it is doubtful if even he clearly understood the scope of the message he was receiving. Sometimes it is very difficult to understand things clearly when we are in the middle of a period of severe testing and turmoil as Jeremiah was in the days before the Babylonians broke through the walls of Jerusalem.

For the whole of his ministry Jeremiah had been giving warnings

---

[1] See Jeremiah 23.19 - 20

that tragedy would overtake the nation unless they remained faithful to God. Many times he had been accused of being a false prophet; that his words were not from the Lord. Now, with the Babylonians at the city gates and all the major cities of Judah in ruins, everyone could see that he was a true prophet that his warnings had indeed come from the throne-room of God.

Jeremiah's emotions must have been tearing him apart. On the one hand there was the fierce exultation that he had been right in giving such strong words of warning to the nation. On the other hand he would have been deeply grieved at the inevitability of judgement and suffering coming upon the people and the nation he loved. Now that God had removed his cover of protection from over the city it was only a matter of time before the enemy broke through the walls to begin their work of murder and destruction. But where was God in all this? Would he allow the nation to be utterly destroyed? Was this to be the end of the Covenant relationship between God and Israel?

These questions must have been in Jeremiah's urgent intercessions in the final days of the city. Was there no hope? Was this the end of Israel? It is at this point that a great revelation came to Jeremiah like a powerful ray of sunlight breaking through the gloom of dark storm clouds. Suddenly he heard the Lord saying to him that he had not forgotten his covenant, but out of this tragedy he would bring a new covenant which would not be like the old covenant with the law written on blocks of stone, but this would be a new covenant in the hearts of God's people. The tragedy that was about to unfold would be a time of re-creation when God would break down the barriers of hatred between the tribes of Israel that for centuries had prevented national unity.

A Message of Hope

The word Jeremiah received was *"At that time, declares the Lord, I will be the God of all the clans of Israel and they will be my people."* This was immediately following the words of warning he had twice given earlier that are recorded in 23.19-20 and 30.23-24, that the anger of the Lord would not turn back until he had fully accomplished the purposes of his heart.

The purposes of God's heart were for unity among his people. *"I will be the God of all the clans of Israel and they will be my people."* This is an amazing statement because the clans and tribes of Israel had been at war with one another ever since the time of Jacob when his sons sold Joseph into slavery in Egypt. Here is Jeremiah prophesying that the destruction of Jerusalem and the exile, which would be a time of great suffering that would take many people into slavery in Babylon, would actually be a time when God would work a miracle of social and spiritual transformation that would heal the ancient divisions among the people of Israel.

The prophecy is that God would bring triumph out of disaster, victory out of defeat, good out of evil, just as Joseph had said to his brothers when they came to buy corn in Egypt and they were terrified that he was going to punish them, saying that what they intended for evil God had turned into good.

Re-uniting the Tribes

This is how God loves to do things. He turns our Calvaries into Gardens of Resurrection and our disasters into new opportunities for the Kingdom. *"The days are coming,"* declares the Lord, *"when I will bring my people Israel and Judah back from captivity and restore them to the land I gave to their forefathers to possess"* Jeremiah 30:3. In the next verse Jeremiah emphasises that God was speaking these words to **both Israel and Judah!**

This is an amazing statement because Jeremiah was a southerner, born into a priestly family in Anathoth some two miles north east of Jerusalem. Today it is a mixed Jewish/Palestinian settlement on the suburban outskirts of Jerusalem. It is doubtful if his family served at the Temple in Jerusalem because they were descendants of Eli and Abiathar who had been banished by King Solomon [2]. They were probably only allowed minor priestly duties and Jeremiah's unpopularity no doubt added to their discomfort and increased their antagonism towards him [3]. He would have grown up surrounded by all the prejudices and attitudes of southern superiority that were current in his day. Very few people in Judah had shed a tear over the demise of Israel in the North when it had been overrun by the Assyrians.

In Jeremiah's day the northern kingdom of Israel no longer existed. Many of its population had been deported and scattered across what we now know as Iraq and Iran. Whole communities

---

[2] See 1 Kings 2.26 - 27

[3] Also see Jeremiah 11.18 - 23

had been brought into Samaria by the Assyrians from other captured territories and settled in Israel. They had already intermarried with the ten tribes of Israel who were despised by Benjamin and Judah in the south, who took pride in their racial purity.

Now they too were facing a similar fate from the Chaldean Empire, and the proud people of Jerusalem were destined for exile in Babylon. Suddenly Jeremiah perceived that God would actually use the impending disaster as a means of working out his own good purposes. *"How awful that day will be! None will be like it. It will be a time of trouble for Jacob, but he will be saved out of it".*

Jeremiah 30.7

One Nation Under God

Many years earlier, in the desert, God had spoken to Moses and used him to bring the tribes out of slavery in Egypt. They were a difficult people to lead, as Moses found to his cost through forty years in the wilderness. They were divided into families, clans and tribes, but God made a covenant with them at Sinai which, despite all the difficulties and tensions, succeeded in making them into one nation under God. It was this unity that enabled Joshua to lead them successfully across the Jordan to possess the land and share it out among the tribes. But their geographical separation from Dan to Be'er Sheva brought back the old tribal divisions.

It was King David who achieved the seemingly impossible. The elders of all the tribes came to him at Hebron after the death of King Saul and asked him to be their leader, which enabled him to rule the whole nation by consent in an atmosphere of trust and unity for the first time in the history of the twelve tribes. There is an interesting account in 1 Chronicles 12 of all the tribes of Israel sending their leading men to David at Hebron when he became king after the death of King Saul.

Most of the tribes sent their experienced soldiers, many of them armed for battle. Some of the tribes sent large numbers of fighting men: 40,000 experienced soldiers came from Asher, 50,000 came from Zebulun, all *"experienced soldiers prepared for battle with every type of weapon"*. 120,000 *"armed with every type of weapon"* came from East of the Jordan. But there was one tribe that sent the smallest number of men, only 200.

For David these men were probably the most valuable to come from any of the tribes. Each had their family life well regulated and in good order; they were the men of Issachar who *"understood the times and knew what Israel should do"* 1 Chronicles 12.32. In the next two chapters we find David conferring with the leaders who had come to him and several times there is the phrase *"David enquired of God"*. You can be sure that this was a corporate exercise of intercession and sharing what they were hearing from the Lord.

When Things Go Wrong

It was this ability to hear from God and to give divine guidance that was so valuable for David's leadership and contributed to bonding the tribes together in unity, with a shared vision, a common mission and a commitment to the Lord God of their fathers.

This national unity was continued under Solomon's leadership. Sadly things went wrong after Solomon's death and the old mistrust arose and the tribal antagonisms broke out. The northerners would not be ruled by the southerners who, they felt, simply wanted to exploit them by levying heavy taxes upon them for their own pleasure and self-aggrandisement.

Jeremiah saw that it was only through national disaster and through exile from the land that the people would forget their old tribal divisions and bitterness and become one nation under God in a time of restoration. This clearly would require an incredible change of heart. He prophesied, *"There will be a day when watchmen cry out on the hills of Ephraim, 'Come, let us go up to Zion, to the Lord our God'"* Jeremiah 31.6

This incredible statement went down like a lead balloon. The impact was something like the outcry that would follow if a Presbyterian minister had stood up in Belfast back in the days of the troubles of the 1970s and prophesied, "The day will come when Ulstermen will no longer wish to maintain their separate Protestant churches in the north but will go on a pilgrimage to Dublin seeking to declare their unity as Irishmen and become one nation under God!" It takes little imagination to picture the effect that such a statement would have had. The whole of Protestant Belfast would have been set alight and the prophet/preacher would have been stoned! That's a little bit like the effect that

Jeremiah's statement would have had in Jerusalem.

Jeremiah's Vision

It was through divine insight that Jeremiah realised that the only way the enmity and strife between the north and south in Israel could be broken would be if God allowed disaster to come upon both communities. This was the only way God could achieve his purposes. That vision of one nation, with no tribal divisions in the land of Israel, remained unfulfilled for 2,500 years until after World War II and the human tragedy of the murder of 6 million Jews in the Holocaust. Jews from all around the world then began re-gathering in the land without even knowing their tribal origins or clans.

But Jeremiah's vision of one nation under God; repenting for having broken the covenant; declaring their total obedience to the word of the Lord; and recognising the everlasting love of God, has yet to be fulfilled, unless this is interpreted as being fulfilled through Jesus the Messiah. The danger of this is that it can lead to 'replacement theology' – the view that the church has replaced Israel in the purposes of God which is a direct denial of Jeremiah 31.31-37. In the same way the prophecy of Isaiah that Israel would become a light for the Gentile nations remains yet to be fully fulfilled. But the word of God never returns to him empty. It accomplishes what he desires and achieves the purposes for which he sends it. [4]

God is still saying to his ancient people Israel with whom he established an everlasting covenant, *"I have loved you with an everlasting love; I have drawn you with loving-kindness"* Jeremiah 31.3. The day will come in God's sovereign timing when Ephraim and Judah will recognise their oneness as God's great love embraces them and they will be drawn into unity – a unity that may also include some of the Arab nations.[5]

This sounds impossible after centuries of hostility and hatred. But God can make impossible things possible. Jeremiah acknowledged this in his great prayer of faith. In his prayer he said, *"Ah Sovereign Lord, you have made the heavens and the earth by your great power and outstretched arm. Nothing is too hard for you".*

Jeremiah 32.17

---

[4] See Isaiah 55.11

[5] See Zechariah 14.16 - 19, Micah 7.12, Amos 9.12

Maybe the unity foreseen by Jeremiah is waiting for God to break down the barriers and establish what Paul describes as 'the one new man' through his New Covenant (foreseen by Jeremiah in 31.31) when the love of God will be shed abroad through the one Name that alone can bring peace and unity to all mankind, the Name of Jesus Messiah.

We have not yet seen any society composed of Jewish and Gentile believers in Jesus similar to the 'one new man' but there is plenty of evidence of the power of the name of Jesus to transform society when his people put their trust fully in him. A recent example of which I am personally aware will suffice to illustrate the point. It occurred in Indonesia in the early 1990s.

National Transformation - Indonesia

I am indebted to my wife for the background to this account which she recorded in her book, *"Rich Christians Poor Christians"*. [6] Indonesia at that time had the largest Muslim population in the world. In the 1960s it was torn apart by civil war when there was an attempt to establish Chinese style Communism in the nation. Some estimates say that up to 1,000,000 people were killed in the conflict as streams and rivers ran with blood.

The Chinese minority of the population were particular targets and old scores among neighbours were settled in the general anarchy. Many of the Chinese were Christians and the way they bore themselves among their neighbours paved the way for large numbers to turn to the Christian faith.

A great spiritual awakening began around this time among peasant farming people on the island of Timor which spread like a prairie fire across many other islands in the wake of the political and social turmoil that had engulfed the whole nation. There were many manifestations of the power of Christ to heal as well as to transform lives. Signs and wonders were performed through simple believers who had the confidence to call upon the name of Jesus to meet every need. Government forces eventually overcame the anarchy and restored order so that the task of reconstructing the nation could begin.

The spiritual awakening materially helped the work of reconstruction by breaking down barriers of fear and mistrust and promoting the

---

[6] Monica Hill, **Rich Christians Poor Christians**, Marshall Pickering, London, 1989, pages 35 - 38

love of Jesus. The gospel began to exercise a reconciling and healing mission in the nation and small church fellowships planted all over the country began to grow into very large congregations numbered in thousands. When the spiritual revival began in 1965 the Christian presence in Indonesia was less than 10%.

Twenty years later the Muslim Government officially estimated that 20% of the population was now Christian. For political reasons, because Indonesia was officially a Muslim country, the Government counted Catholics separately and they estimated that a further 20% of the population was Catholic. By the early 1990s the Government was becoming increasingly alarmed by the success of evangelical missions that were attracting large numbers to their meetings and seeing an enormous growth in the Christian community.

The Government then decided upon a policy of population transmigration that would have both social and religious benefit. Jakarta was greatly overcrowded; unemployment and poverty was rife, so too was social unrest. The transmigration policy targeted Muslim families in the worst areas of unemployment and social deprivation and moved them to islands where there was 100% Christian population in the hope that this would not only improve their socio-economic situation but also impact the religious balance.

In the event the Christian families welcomed their new neighbours and made every effort to help them to relocate and to integrate into the local community. The new families were overwhelmed with the love and generosity they were shown and large numbers converted to Christianity. From the Government's standpoint the whole transmigration policy was a disaster and within 10 years it was dropped. Far from helping to create a balance of the two major religions the population movement had simply provided fertile ground for Christian evangelism.

From the Christian standpoint this, of course, is a good example of how evangelism should work - not with specially planned missions and programmes, but simply through the witness of ordinary Christians practising their faith: acting in such a way that the love of God could be clearly seen at work in the community.

National Transformation - Israel and Judah

Jeremiah was looking for national transformation but he knew that the only way it could happen would not be through human activity but through God's sovereign intervention and the exercise of his divine power. The promise of this is recorded in Jeremiah chapters 30 to 33 which are known as the "Book of Consolation". They represent a turning point in the ministry of the prophet.

With the Babylonian army about to break through the defences of Jerusalem, Jeremiah sensed the grief in God's heart that accorded with the great fear and sorrow that he himself was experiencing. He was imprisoned in the guard house of the Royal Palace and was powerless to do anything to influence the situation. Nothing could now stop the tragedy that was about to unfold, but then he had a dream that he realised was actually a prophetic vision in which he had foreseen the unfolding of the purposes of God for his covenant people.

In the vision he saw a great throng of people coming back to the land after exile. *"Among them will be the blind and the lame, expectant mothers and women in labour".*   Jeremiah 31.8

Jeremiah had a great heart for the people of the northern kingdom of Israel who had been scattered across the Assyrian Empire and were despised by the smug southerners of Judah and especially by the ruling aristocrats in Jerusalem. He may have had a special sympathy for the northerners because he himself came from a family that had been despised since they had been rejected by King Solomon. [7]

There is clearly grief in Jeremiah's voice as he reports *"A voice is heard in Ramah, mourning and great weeping, Rachel weeping for her children and refusing to be comforted."* This is followed by the declaration *"They will return from the land of the enemy. So there is hope for your future… Is not Ephraim my dear son, the child in whom I delight? Though I often speak against him, I still remember him. Therefore my heart yearns for him; I have great compassion for him, declares the Lord".*   Jeremiah 31.20

This is followed by a further reference to "virgin Israel" which shows that God is already seeing his people cleansed and redeemed returning to the land. But he also includes the people of Judah and this is the central theme of these chapters – that God

---

[7] see 1 Kings 2.26 - 27

will re-unite the broken tribes of Israel and establish an everlasting covenant with them that will be written on their hearts.

The central pronouncement is in Jeremiah 31.27-28, which is a pivotal point in the whole message of Jeremiah and a turning point in his ministry. It represents a reversal of the commission he was given at the beginning of his ministry[8]. *"The days are coming, declares the Lord, when I will plant the house of Israel and the house of Judah with the offspring of men and of animals. Just as I watched over them to uproot and tear down, and to overflow, destroy and bring disaster, so I will watch over them to build and to plant, declares the Lord."* Jeremiah was seeing that the only way in which the Lord could work out his purposes through his unfaithful people was to allow them to go through the tragedy of banishment from the land and then to redeem them from slavery as he had done when they were in Egypt.

In order to confirm the certainty of this promise of restoration God sent Jeremiah a sign that was unmistakable. His cousin, Hanamel, came to him telling him that it was his right to buy a field in Anathoth as part of his family's inheritance. The field was already in enemy occupied territory and so was probably worthless but Jeremiah solemnly weighed out 17 shekels of silver and signed the deed of purchase plus a sealed copy ensuring that the field now legally belonged to him. It was a significant moment in which Jeremiah expressed his confidence in the promise of restoration that he was hearing from God.

Before signing this deed Jeremiah spent a long time in urgent intercession before the Lord to make sure that he was correctly hearing this momentous message of God's unchanging love for his people. He was assured,

"I am the Lord, the God of all mankind. Is anything too hard for me? Therefore, this is what the Lord says: I am about to hand this city over to the Babylonians and to Nebuchadnezzar king of Babylon, who will capture it. The Babylonians who are attacking this city will come in and set it on fire; they will burn it down, along with the houses where the people provoked me to anger by burning incense on the roofs to Baal and by pouring out drink offerings to other gods. The people of Israel and Judah have done nothing but evil in my sight from their youth...

---

[8] see Jeremiah 1.10

"Nevertheless, I will bring health and healing to it; I will heal my people and let them enjoy abundant peace and security. I will bring Judah and Israel back from captivity and will rebuild them as they were before. I will cleanse them from all the sins they have committed against me and will forgive all their sins and rebellion against me".   Jeremiah 32.27 - 29; 33.6 - 8

Jeremiah lived through the terrible days of destruction as the city fell to the Babylonians, but he did not live to see the time of restoration except through the eyes of faith. The final words of the 'Book of Consolation' confirm God's unbreakable love that survives all human tragedies with the solemn promise to reunite the scattered people of Israel and Judah. *"I will restore their fortunes and have compassion on them".*   Jeremiah 33.26

Chapter Eight

GOD'S LOVE FOR THE ALIEN AND OUTCAST

This chapter highlights Isaiah 56 with its beautiful message of God's love for the alien and the outcast climaxing in the declaration "My house will be called a house of prayer for all nations". *It also notes how Israel failed to understand and implement this message.*

Meeting a Rabbi

The plane leaving Tel Aviv for London was full. Monica and I had been leading a party on a study trip around Israel. It was just after the end of Passover so there was quite a large number of Orthodox Jews on the plane who had been to Israel for the celebration. There was the usual jostling for seats in the Orthodox party with increasing agitation among the cabin crew who were anxious to get everyone seated for takeoff so that we did not miss our flight slot.

Eventually everyone was seated and one of them sat beside me. I had a strong feeling from the way others were addressing him that he was a rabbi. I wanted to get into conversation with him so after a while I opened my Bible and began reading in Isaiah. I knew this would make him curious. After a while he could contain himself no longer and he turned to me and whispered, "Are you a Jew?" I said, "No I'm not, but I love your Scriptures."

Within moments we were in deep conversation. He told me that he was the senior rabbi of a North London Synagogue, one that I knew quite well from the years that I'd spent in pastoral ministry in Tottenham. We had a lot in common as we both knew that area quite well and we both had a good knowledge of Israel and of the biblical history of Israel. But I became increasingly amazed at his lack of knowledge of the prophets of Israel. He confessed that he hardly ever read the Prophets and I found myself expounding the Book of Isaiah to him.

I focused on the chapters that were directed to the exiles in Babylon and particularly to the message of Isaiah 56, which was entirely new to him. He couldn't deny that it was the word of the Lord but its message clearly made him uncomfortable. It paved the way for me to turn to Isaiah 53 beginning with the fourth Servant Song at Isaiah 52.13. This was completely new territory for him and I don't think he knew the existence of the Servant Songs.[1]

I've often prayed for that rabbi since that encounter and wondered what effect it had upon him: if it moved him to do his own reading in Isaiah and to think about Jesus. I wondered if he was now a secret believer like a number of rabbis in Israel. Perhaps Jesus had appeared to him as he did to Saul on the road to Damascus and as he has done to thousands of Israelis in the modern State of Israel where more than half of all believers in Jesus are said to have come to faith by revelation rather than through evangelism.

An Important Message

The message of Isaiah 56 that I used in my conversation with the rabbi is one of the most significant chapters in any of the prophets of Israel. The historical background is important if we are to gain an understanding of the message which gives an amazingly fresh insight into the love of God. It begins, *"This is what the Lord says: maintain justice and do what is right, for my salvation is close at hand and my justice will soon be revealed"*.   Isaiah 56.1

These words were specifically addressed to the people of Judah who were in exile in Babylon. It was at a time very near the end of the exile that Jeremiah had said would last some 70 years. It is quite possible that Cyrus had already taken Babylon and Isaiah was now encouraging the exiles to get ready to leave.

The prophet was given the task of preparing the people for the return to the land of their fathers and the rebuilding of Jerusalem from the ruins of destruction and the years of neglect and decay. The exiles were in no condition to undertake such a tremendous responsibility. Most of those hearing the message of the prophet had been born in captivity and only knew of their homeland through the tales (or laments) of their fathers.

---

[1] see note on page 143 chapter 9

Creation and Covenant

Even their basic understanding of God was deficient, so in bringing the announcement of the forthcoming breaking of the power of Babylon the prophetic task had been first to explain to the people who God was. They had to be convinced that the God of their fathers, the God of Abraham, Isaac and Jacob, was in fact the Creator of the Universe who held the nations in his hands *"as a drop in a bucket"*.   Isaiah 40.15

The prophet then had to remind them of the covenant that God had made with Israel and that God was a covenant-keeping God who was now about to fulfil his promises and to demonstrate his unbreakable love for his people despite their unfaithfulness which had resulted in the exile. The message of the prophet was that the people would return to the land of Israel redeemed by the Lord both physically and spiritually.

Their physical redemption was going to be accomplished by God using a pagan ruler, Cyrus, to overthrow the power of Babylon and release his covenant people from slavery. The spiritual redemption would be accomplished by the recognition that this new act of God's saving his people would be on a par with what he did for their forefathers in the time of Moses to break the power of Egypt and to release his people from bondage. This spiritual redemption would renew their faith in God and give them new understanding of his unbreakable love and the way he acts to fulfil his covenant promises, which is a demonstration of his 'justice'. [2]

Purpose of the Covenant

Isaiah also had to explain the purpose underlying the covenant that God had established with the patriarchs of Israel. He said

"I, the Lord, have called you in justice; I will take hold of your hand. I will keep you and make you to be a covenant for the people and a light for the Gentiles, to open eyes that are blind, to free captives from prison and to release from the dungeon those who sit in darkness".   Isaiah 42.6 - 7

This is a statement of tremendous importance that explains the nature of the servanthood of Israel who were chosen by God to be the means through whom he would reveal his nature and purposes

---

[2] This understanding of 'justice' is dealt with in Chapter 11

117

to the other nations; taking light to the Gentile nations; giving understanding to people who were spiritually blind and actually releasing those who were under the curse of death.

This was the whole purpose of God's covenant calling - to bring salvation to all humanity - to enable people of all nations to come into a right relationship with God the Creator of the Universe. This would also create right relationships on a human level and bring peace to the warring tribes and nations who were hostile to each other. This was the covenant of peace that God was establishing, which had been wonderfully foreseen 200 years earlier by both Isaiah of Jerusalem and the prophet Micah each of whom had spoken of the word of the Lord going out from Jerusalem. This would teach the nations the way of the Lord and enable them to walk in his paths, which would result in beating swords into ploughshares and nations no longer taking up the sword against other nations or training for war any more. [3]

This revelation of God was the task that God had eternally planned for Israel and the reason why he had established the covenant with the patriarchs. So far this purpose had never been understood or fulfilled by Israel. Now that God was about to give his people a second chance by freeing them from captivity and taking them back to the land of promise, he had to prepare them. It was essential that in returning they would not simply drop into the old ways of spiritual idolatry and narrow-minded concentration upon the acquisition of power, physical prosperity and wealth.

The returning exiles, if they were to be a company of redeemed, had to understand God's purpose in calling them into a special relationship with himself. That was the objective of Isaiah chapter 56 - expounding the purpose of God's calling to the nation of Israel. That calling is still not understood in Israel and this was what I had tried to expound to the Rabbi on the plane to London. It is my belief that before Israel can accept the mission of Messiah Jesus, her people have to understand Israel's own calling by God which is clearly set out in the message of the prophets and is particularly seen in Isaiah 56.

[3] See Isaiah 2.1-4 and Micah 4.1-5

Covenant Requirements

There were just three requirements for the blessing of God to be upon all the people who returned from Babylon to Jerusalem. The first was to maintain justice. Maintaining a right relationship with God and with other human beings was of the first importance - far more important than the observation of religious practices. All the prophets disliked religion, especially where it was a substitute for right relationships. Hence Amos had thundered a word from the Lord some two centuries earlier, *"I hate, I despise your religious feasts; I cannot stand your assemblies... away with the noise of your songs! I will not listen to the music of your harps. But let justice roll on like a river".*   Amos 5.21 - 24

The second was to observe the Sabbath. This was important to give everyone the opportunity to be released from the demands of work, of making a living, and to have the opportunity of thinking about the word of the Lord; reflecting upon spiritual things rather than simply being driven by physical demands.The third requirement was simply refraining from doing evil.

Foreigners and Eunuchs Included!

No one would have seen anything remarkable in those three requirements but the next word would have left most of the exiles speechless with amazement. *"Let no foreigner who has bound himself to the Lord say, the Lord will surely exclude me from his people, and let not any eunuch complain, I am only a dry tree."* Isaiah 56.3. Both foreigners and eunuchs were forbidden to enter the temple, so they were excluded from the worship of God. The foreigner was excluded by birth and the eunuch because his body had been emasculated. The law stated, *"No one who has been emasculated by crushing or cutting may enter the assembly of the Lord".*   Deuteronomy 23.1

Isaiah was foreseeing the rebuilding of the temple by the returning exiles, a number of whom would have been forcibly castrated by the Babylonians so that they could serve as slaves in the royal household or in places where they would come into contact with women. Clearly, it was not right that they should be banned from worshipping the Lord, but because this new regulation was contrary to those given by Moses, the Prophet adds,

"For this is what the Lord says".

But in order to show the love and compassion of God and that this was not just a change of regulations for expediency it is stated as a fresh revelation from God. *"To the eunuchs who keep my Sabbaths, who choose what pleases me and hold fast to my covenant - to them I will give within my temple and its walls a memorial and a name better than sons and daughters; I will give them an everlasting name that will not be cut off."* Isaiah 56.4 -5

This is a revolutionary statement that shows the overwhelming love of God. Eunuchs were unable to have children and in ancient Israel men were thought to live on through their children. In this promise God gives a solemn undertaking that such a man, provided he chooses to hold fast to the Lord, would be given a special place in the company of God's people. A memorial would be erected bearing his name actually within the walls of the temple, so that his name would always be there in a place of honour, which would actually be better than having children to continue his name. He would have an everlasting name that would not be cut off: which would always be, symbolically, in the presence of the Lord.

It was probably even more amazing for the exiles, especially the older ones who knew the Mosaic regulations, to hear that *"foreigners who bind themselves to the Lord to serve him, to love the name of the Lord, and to worship him"* Isaiah 56.7. would be allowed on the holy Temple Mount and would even be welcome to worship in the temple itself. The solemn promise of God was to *"give them joy in my house of prayer"* - and, even more amazingly, - their offerings would be acceptable upon the altar in the temple. In order to ram home the significance of this revolutionary statement it was followed by the promise, *"For my house will be called a house of prayer for all nations".* [4] Isaiah 56.7

House of Prayer

This would be a paradigm shift in the religious practices of Israel because hitherto the major activities in the temple had revolved around animal sacrifice. The prophecy said that God was calling for his house to be primarily a ***place of prayer!*** But not only for the Hebrew people - ***also for the Gentiles!***

---

[4] See also Luke 19.45 where Jesus quotes this verse when he was cleansing the temple of merchants.

These were two mega changes in the spiritual life of Israel that the prophet was foretelling.

But they did not happen. Later in this chapter we will deal with the historic reasons why this teaching which Isaiah brought as a word from God was never accepted. But first we fast-track forward 500 years to the time when Jesus used this prophecy in his ministry.

When he entered the court of the Gentiles Jesus found it crowded with cattle and merchants. This was the only part of the temple where Gentiles were allowed so there was no possibility of the Gentiles being able to worship God – in the atmosphere of a busy market.

Historically there should have been an altar there outside the restricted area of the temple. It was known as the 'altar of witness' that had been there from the early days of the first temple constructed by Solomon, although there had been times when it had been neglected; as in the time of King Asa when it is recorded, *"He repaired the altar of the Lord that was in front of the portico of the Lord's temple"*, which triggered a major spiritual revival that reached people, including aliens, far beyond the borders of Judah.[5]

Jesus drove out the cattle and overturned the moneychangers' tables quoting the word from Isaiah, *"My house shall be called a house of prayer for all nations"* Mark 11.17. Modern preachers often attribute Jesus' indignation to the commercialisation of the temple. But his use of this quotation has a far greater significance in which Jesus is identifying with the call for the temple to be a place where people from all nations could come and seek the presence of God. Here, in the outer court, was the only place Gentiles could pray in the temple and it was being denied to them.

These words in Isaiah 56 were revolutionary. They were an expression of God's intention to use the redeemed people of Israel as his servant. Those who returned to the Promised Land after the exile would be a spiritually renewed people capable of fulfilling God's covenant purposes. Sadly, as foreseen in the fourth Servant Song,[6] it was not Israel as a nation that would fulfil the purposes of God but an individual Servant. Out of the nation there would come One who, in his own Person, would be the instrument

---

[5] See 2 Chronicles 15.8

[6] See Chapter 9

of salvation for many; the One who would break the curse of death over the whole of humanity.

What went wrong? Why could the nation of Israel not fulfil the covenant purposes of God? The revelation given to Isaiah was perfectly clear. Israel, as God's covenant people, were to be the bearers of light for the Gentile nations and the new temple would be a place where all nations would be welcome to worship the Lord. It would be a place from which the word of the Lord and his teaching would go out to all nations so that people of all nations could know him and come into a right relationship with him [7]. This was God's intention for his people whom he had called to be his servant and through whom it was his purpose to reveal his nature and purposes to all peoples. But this was neither understood nor accepted.

Isaiah's Prophecy Rejected

What may be seen as a turning point in world history occurred in the year 458 BC. It was the year that the word of the Lord recorded in Isaiah 56 was abrogated.

The first generation of returned exiles had a difficult time. The great enthusiasm with which they returned dissipated in the harsh reality of destruction that confronted them. Everywhere was devastation; in the city; in the townships; in the villages and in the countryside. The land had been neglected for decades and it was difficult to scrape a living from the soil. Industry and commerce were non-existent. The economy, like the land, was bankrupt. Life for that first generation was extremely hard - even just providing the basic necessities of food and shelter.

Haggai was the first of the post-exilic prophets to scold the people severely. *"Give careful thought to your ways,"* he said. *"You have planted much, but have harvested little. You eat, but you never have enough. You drink, but never have your fill. You put on clothes, but you are not warm. You earn wages, only to put them in a purse with holes in it."*

Haggai 1.5 - 6

He upbraided them for having built their own houses but not having built the house of the Lord. They had concentrated on rebuilding the commercial and social structures but had neglected the spiritual life of the nation.

---

[7] Isaiah 2 and Micah 4

Cyrus had overthrown the Babylonian Empire in 538 BC and he immediately issued an edict releasing the people of Judah from slavery in the city. The following year the first trickle of Judeans began returning to Jerusalem. Sometime within the next five years a large transmigration took place. Their family names are listed in Ezra 2 where it is recorded that, *"The whole company numbered 42,360, besides their 7,337 menservants and maidservants."* This is very much larger than the small company of 4,600 taken into slavery from Jerusalem to Babylon according to Jeremiah 52.30.[8] Clearly, they were not returning as slaves but as a prosperous company triumphantly returning to their homeland.

Many families were sufficiently wealthy to have servants in attendance. They also had a choir of 200 men and women to lead the singing which turned the whole migration into a pilgrimage. Ezra also records that they had 736 horses, 245 mules, 435 camels and 6,720 donkeys! They were certainly not like the bedraggled dispirited company that had left Jerusalem. They had heeded Jeremiah's advice to settle down, build houses, encourage their children to marry and have children and engage in the life of the city. Clearly they had done this to great advantage because when they arrived back in Jerusalem they took a freewill offering for the temple rebuilding fund that amounted to about 500 kg of gold and 2 $\frac{1}{2}$ tons of silver. No wonder they needed all those mules!

Life was extremely hard for this first generation of returnees especially those who had been used to a life of luxury in Babylon. They rebuilt the altar in the ruins of the temple where it once stood so that the morning and evening sacrifices and prayers could be re-established and they even laid the foundation stone for the temple. But that was as far as they went.

Ezra records that there was opposition from local people - the Samaritans who had spread across the land after the departure of the Judeans - but the explanation given by Haggai probably more accurately reflects the situation. He says that the people were fully occupied building their own houses and re-establishing the social and economic life of the nation. But even though they devoted all their days to rebuilding the nation their efforts did not bring prosperity. It must have been particularly

---

[8] See Chapter 5 page 79

hard for people who had grand houses and servants in Babylon to be reduced to this kind of hard labour back in Israel.

People responded to Haggai's rebuke in the year 520 BC. They immediately began rebuilding the temple and it was finished within six years - dedicated in 515 BC. But although Haggai had said that rebuilding the temple would turn the fortunes of the nation, life continued to be very hard throughout the lifetime of the former exiles. The walls of Jerusalem had never been rebuilt; it was a sorry sight for passers-by to see the ruins of the once proud city and centre of commerce. People became more and more dispirited and simply concentrated upon survival, living with their own families without concern for the good of the nation. That was the situation some 60 years after Haggai's words had stirred them to action. It was at this point in the year 458 BC that a newcomer arrived from Persia - Ezra the priest.

He came from a long line of Orthodox priests going back to Phineas and had spent his life studying the regulations in the code of Moses [9].

Ultra-Orthodox Priest

Ezra had evidently convinced the Emperor Artaxerxes that he and his sons were in danger of the wrath of God because the newly rebuilt temple in Jerusalem lacked the articles for worship that had been looted by the Babylonians back in 596 BC and were still in Babylon. The Emperor gave Ezra a letter empowering him to take anything that he wanted, including gold from the royal treasury. He was to go back to Jerusalem with all the articles he could discover and ensure the worship of God was properly carried out.

He was even given authority to supervise civil administration by appointing magistrates and judges, and to ensure that everyone worshipped God in the prescribed manner. *"Whoever does not obey the law of your God and the Lord the King must surely be punished by death, banishment, confiscation of property, or imprisonment."*

Ezra 7.26

Ezra was the forerunner of the ultra-orthodox Jews of today. He soon discovered that many of the returned exiles had intermarried with local families among the Samaritans. He recorded, *"They have taken some of their daughters as wives*

---

[9] See Ezra 7.10

for themselves and their sons, and have mingled the holy race with people around them" Ezra 9.2. This statement, of course, would not be acceptable in the social environment created by our modern equality laws but its significance needs to be seen in the context of the word of God that was current at that time.

For this we must return to Isaiah 56 with which we began this chapter. It was a word addressed to the exiles in Babylon around the time of the conquest by Cyrus, when the prophet was preparing the people for the great act of deliverance that God was about to bring to them that would establish a new era in the relationship between God and his covenant people. This word is of such great importance for understanding the significance of events in this period that it needs to be read as a whole before returning to the scene in Jerusalem that Ezra was addressing in 458 BC.

"This is what the Lord says: Maintain justice and do what is right, for my salvation is close at hand and my justice will soon be revealed. Blessed is the man who does this, the man who holds it fast, who keeps the sabbath without desecrating it, and keeps his hand from doing any evil. Let no foreigner who has bound himself to the Lord say, 'The Lord will surely exclude me from his people'. And let not any eunuch complain 'I am only a dry tree'.

"For this is what the Lord says: the eunuchs who keep my sabbaths, who choose what pleases me and hold fast to my covenant - to them I will give within my temple and its walls a memorial and a name better than sons and daughters; I will give them an everlasting name that will not be cut off.

"And foreigners who bind themselves to the Lord to serve him, to love the name of the Lord, and to worship him, all who keep the Sabbath without desecrating it and who hold fast to my covenant - these I will bring to my holy mountain and give them joy in my house of prayer. Their burnt offerings and sacrifices will be acceptable on my altar; for my house would be called a house of prayer for all nations." Isaiah 56.1 - 4

Ezra made an enormous scene when he heard of the inter-marriage with Samaritans whom he considered racially impure because they were from the northern tribes of Israel among whom the Assyrians had forcibly settled conquered people from other lands. Ezra tore his clothes and tore out the hair from his head and beard. Then when he had gathered a large crowd he began *"weeping and throwing himself down before the house of God."* Ezra 10.1. He said that the reason there was still no great prosperity in the land was because God was punishing them for their sins, *"What has happened to us is the result of our evil deeds and our great guilt."* Ezra 9.13

Someone then suggested to Ezra that they should make a covenant before God to send away all the non-Hebrew women and children. Ezra seized upon this and sent a proclamation out throughout Jerusalem and Judah for all the exiles to assemble in Jerusalem. Three days later they came and stood in the square outside the temple, but it was raining heavily and they were all distressed and in no condition to discuss a serious proposition.

They nevertheless took the decision urged upon them by Ezra that would have lasting significance for Israel and for world history. *"Ezra the priest stood up and said to them, 'You have been unfaithful; you have married foreign women, adding to Israel's guilt. Now make confession to the Lord, the God of your fathers, and do his will. Separate yourselves from the peoples around you and from your foreign wives'."* The whole assembly agreed, *"You are right! We must do as you say."* Ezra 10.10 - 12

This decision was opposed by four leading citizens, one of whom was a Levite - Jonathan, Jahzeiah, Meshullam and Shabbethai, the Levite.[10] We are not told the reasons for their opposition, but the ministry of Isaiah in Babylon was still fresh in the memory of the exile community who had resettled in Judah. It had made a tremendous impression upon the exiles in preparing the way for their return to the land of their fathers. It would be reasonable to conclude that the stand taken by these four men would have been based upon Isaiah's teaching.

Nevertheless, Ezra persuaded all the men to abandon their wives and children and drive them away despite the promises given in Isaiah 56 regarding foreigners who had pledged themselves to the Lord. So, instead of the men of Israel teaching their wives and children to know God and to love the Lord, they drove them out, leaving them without support; breaking the covenant promises of marriage they had made and consigning these women and children to an unknown fate.

---

[10] See Ezra 10.15

Racial Superiority

This racial superiority and exclusivity that was the driving force behind Ezra's racist attitude was the very opposite of the spirit of the 'redeemed of the Lord' envisaged in Isaiah chapter 56 and ran counter to the promise, *"I will also make you a light for the Gentiles, that you may bring my salvation to the ends of the earth"* Isaiah 49.6. The unbreakable love which was God's intention to reveal to the world through his covenant people, spiritually renewed through the experience of exile, was broken in that square in front of the temple in the centre of Jerusalem. The message of God's love that he intended to lavish, not only upon his covenant people, but also to reveal it to all nations, was frustrated.

That was a milestone in world history. Racially segregated Israel was unable to fulfil the purposes of God to be a light for the nations. It was this tragedy that Isaiah was foreseeing in the fourth Servant Song, which is the subject of the next chapter. The world had to await the right time for God to send his Messiah as the Servant of the Lord to accomplish his purposes of bringing salvation to all people. That time came when Rome had broken down national barriers and made travel possible throughout the region, and Greece had provided the world with a common language of communication.

In the fullness of time – *"the Word became flesh."*   John 1.14

Chapter Nine

GOD'S LOVE TRIUMPHS OVER DEATH

This chapter is all about the supreme revelation of God as a God of love seen in the Fourth Servant Song with its beautiful message of the transforming power of God's love that conquers death in order to bring us into a close and intimate relationship with God.

The Fourth Servant Song

"See, my servant will act wisely; he will be raised and lifted up and highly exalted. Just as there were many who were appalled at him - his appearance was so disfigured beyond that of any man and his form marred beyond human likeness - so will he sprinkle many nations, and kings will shut their mouths because of him. For what they were not told, they will see, and what they have not heard, they will understand.

"Who has believed our message and to whom has the arm of the Lord been revealed? He grew up before him like a tender shoot, and like a root out of dry ground. He had no beauty or majesty to attract us to him, nothing in his appearance that we should desire him. He was despised and rejected by men, a man of sorrows, and familiar with suffering. Like one from whom men hide their faces he was despised, and we esteemed him not.

"Surely he took up our infirmities and carried our sorrows, yet we considered him stricken by God, smitten by him, and afflicted. But he was pierced for our transgressions, he was crushed for our iniquities; the punishment that brought us peace was upon him, and by his wounds we are healed. We all, like sheep, have gone astray, each of us has turned to his own way; and the Lord has laid on him the iniquity of us all.

"He was oppressed and afflicted, yet he did not open his mouth; he was led like a lamb to the slaughter, and as a sheep before her shearers is silent, so he did not open his mouth. By oppression and judgement he was taken away. And who *can speak of his descendants? For he was cut off from the land of the living; for the transgression of my people he was stricken. He was assigned a grave with the wicked, and with the rich in his death, though he had done no violence, nor was any deceit in his mouth.*

"Yet it was the Lord's will to crush him and cause him to suffer, and though the Lord makes his life a guilt offering, he will see his offspring and prolong his days, and the will of the Lord will prosper in his hand. After the suffering of his soul, he will see the light of life, and be satisfied; by his knowledge my righteous servant will justify many, and he will bear their iniquities. Therefore I will give him a portion among the great, and he will divide the spoils with the strong, because he poured out his life unto death, and was numbered with the transgressors. For he bore the sin of many, and made intercession for the transgressors."   Isaiah 52.13 - 53.12

Revealing the Nature of God

This final Servant Song is probably the most important announcement in all the utterances of the Hebrew prophets. Our purpose is not to undertake a detailed commentary on the Song but to add to our knowledge of the way the writing Prophets of Israel portrayed the love of God. This great song of lamentation is a statement of how God was intending to deal with the sinfulness of human beings which separates them from each other and from him. In order to understand this we have to remember, as we have already said, that the basic mission of the Prophets was to reveal the nature and purposes of God.

God had called Israel into a covenant relationship with himself precisely so that through them he could be made known to the world. They were to be a light for the nations. For the Prophets, the starting point of revelation was always in what they described as "the deeds of the Lord" - what he had actually done - so the history of God's dealings with his covenant people was recited time and again because therein was revealed not only his purposes but also, most importantly, aspects of his nature.

The supreme revelation was that God was a God of love. He loved his people so much that he would go to any lengths to save them from the consequences of their own sinful nature even when they had got themselves into the most appalling bondage and degradation as when the whole nation was in slavery in Egypt. God showed his great love for the poor, the powerless and the most oppressed of humanity by responding to their cries for help and intervening to break the bondage of the oppressors. By destroying the pursuing Egyptian army and releasing his people God showed his justice as well as his love.

Much had happened since the crossing of the Red Sea, the forty years in the wilderness and the crossing of the Jordan into the Promised Land. Now, the covenant people were once again in slavery, under a new oppressor, Babylon. But God, who was a covenant-keeping God, was about to demonstrate his love and faithfulness by once again releasing his people from slavery. Isaiah records this announcement in chapter 43 where God reminds them of how he had redeemed them from slavery in Egypt and then immediately he says "Forget it!!" - *"Forget the former things; do not dwell in the past. See, I am doing a new thing!"* Isaiah 43.18-19. The new thing would be in preparation for the forthcoming Messianic Age when God would pour out his Spirit upon their descendants.[1]

The Mission of Messiah

In this final Servant Song the means by which God would accomplish this 'new thing' is made clear in the mission of the Messiah which would be completely different from any regular human expectations. The 'Anointed One' whom God would raise up would be highly exalted worldwide, but this would amaze everyone; in fact the rulers of the nations would be speechless, because it would completely turn upside down all their values and preconceptions. Instead of being a fine upstanding attractive human being, his body would be appallingly disfigured, and he would be despised and rejected by people who would rather hide their faces than look at him. This, of course, is exactly what happened when they crucified Jesus, which was the cruellest and most revolting form of death that could be inflicted upon a human body at that time.

After describing the suffering of the Servant, a most surprising announcement is made which suddenly switches the scene from the Servant to ourselves - *"Surely he took up **our** infirmities and carried our sorrows, yet **we** considered him stricken by God."*

---

[1] See Isaiah 44.3

In those days it was a common belief among adherents of all religions that suffering was inflicted by the gods upon the wicked; upon those who had offended the requirements of their god. That is blown away by this astonishing statement that the Servant of God would suffer, not for his own sins, but for ours! They were familiar with the goat bearing the sins of the nation being driven out into the wilderness,[2] but a human being willingly bearing the sins of the people was unknown.

A generation earlier, in the days before the destruction of Jerusalem, Jeremiah had roundly condemned human sacrifice to which the people had turned in their desperation.[3] But a righteous man vicariously taking upon himself the iniquities of others would have been quite incomprehensible to those who heard the pronouncements of the prophet, but we have the advantage of hindsight, being those who already know the mission of Messiah, the Anointed One, the Servant of God in the person of Jesus. It is here that the New Testament enables us to interpret this final Servant Song.

The Meaning of Grace

In writing to Timothy, Paul challenges traditional attitudes towards suffering. He urges Timothy not to be ashamed to speak publicly about the Lord Jesus or to be ashamed that he (Paul) was in prison. He says *"Join with me in suffering for the gospel, by the power of God, who has saved us and called us to a holy life - not because of anything we have done but because of his own purpose and grace"* 2 Timothy 1.8-9. This is an important statement that enables us to understand Isaiah's Servant Song because Paul was well versed in Hebrew theology. He was an academic who had been taught by Rabbi Gamaliel. So he was familiar with the teaching of the prophets that God's love for his people is unconditional and it is not something we earn.

That is what "Grace" is all about. It is the unmerited love of God lavished upon his people and especially extended to the poor,

---

[2] Yom Kippur was the most solemn and important day in the biblical calendar. It was the only day in the year when any Israelite was permitted to enter the Holy of Holies in the temple. The High Priest had to perform a number of sacrifices to atone for his own sins and the sins of the people. A goat was then led outside the city and driven into the wilderness, symbolically taking the sins of the people with it. The High Priest was then able to enter the Holy of Holies, sprinkle blood on the Ark of the Covenant, and then go outside, lifting his hands to pronounce the Aaronic blessing over the people.

[3] See Jeremiah 7.31

the oppressed and the downtrodden because they are the most in need. That does not mean that God has favourites but simply that he recognises the special need of people at different times in their lives.

A mother of a large family was once asked which of her children she loved the most. She replied, "The one who is sick until he is better; the one who is having problems with school friends until relationships are healed; the one who is away until he comes home". She was simply recognising the special needs of each of her family and her love, while equally distributed, was lavished upon the one with special needs. God, who is at least as good as the most loving parent, while loving all his children without favour, lavishes his love upon those who have a special need.

This is how the prophets used the accounts of God's goodness to Israel in the history of the nation and this is why the Passover is still celebrated today in Jewish homes because it tells the story of God's grace; his unmerited love for his children when they were in deepest trouble. In Egypt in the time of Moses they were utterly powerless to help themselves; they were totally unable to break the power of the oppressors who had enslaved them but when they cried out to the God of their fathers he acted in accordance with his promise to Abraham because he is faithful and never breaks his promise.

It was not that the Hebrew slaves had earned God's love or that they deserved to be set free; it was simply that God loved them so much that he responded to their cries for help. It is this same principle, learnt from the teaching of the prophets, which lay behind Paul's statement that Christ died for us while we were still sinners. We hadn't earned his love; it was entirely unmerited, but this is the teaching of the New Testament that we can take back to Isaiah's Servant Song to give us fresh understanding.

Defining Justice

Much of our difficulty in understanding statements such as *"he was pierced for our transgressions, he was crushed for our iniquities"* Isaiah 53.5 lies in our failure to understand the nature of God as revealed in the teaching of the prophets. They perceived that God is a God of justice who lavishes his love upon those who are totally undeserving and that this was a demonstration, not of God's mercy, but of his *justice!* This not only enriches our understanding of the love of God, but it also provides a definitive Hebraic understanding of 'justice' which contrasts sharply with our Western understanding.

Those who receive the love of God are often unable immediately to return his love due to their circumstances. They can only receive; they have nothing to give in return. It is rather like the rough-sleeping homeless man whom I encountered in Trafalgar Square, recounted in Chapter One. In a spontaneous outpouring of the love of God I was able to embrace him. He had nothing to give in return except, through tears, to accept what was freely offered.

Our problem in understanding the love of God is that we see it through the kaleidoscope of Western culture. Even our understanding of the New Testament is moulded by Greek and Latin concepts rather than Hebraic. The most obvious errors arise through our failure to understand the Hebraic concept of the 'justice of God' as seen through the prophets.[4] In our Western culture we can understand that God's love towards undeserving people is an act of mercy but we cannot understand how it is a demonstration of God's *justice.* This is because our Western mindset has been moulded by Roman law, which decreed that justice demanded that every offender should receive the punishment that exactly fitted his crime. That is what is known as 'distributive justice': giving everyone what they deserve.

There is plenty of evidence of distributive justice being exercised in ancient Israel but it was never part of the teaching of the prophets. Distributive justice is part of the Mosaic regulations for maintaining order in society. Exodus 21 gives a number of practical examples where the actions of an offender demand

---

[4] There are three references in Isaiah which suggest God exercising distributive justice against the enemies of Israel, such as *"For the Lord has a day of vengeance, a year of retribution, to uphold Zion's cause"* (Isaiah 34.8) similarly in the next chapter it is stated, *"Be strong, do not fear; your God will come, he will come with vengeance; with divine retribution he will come to save you."* (35.4) both of these statements are in the form of apocalyptic poetry expressing God's purpose of salvation for his people through which he will change their circumstances from oppression to blessing. The third reference is in Isaiah 59.18. The text in all the most reliable manuscripts is virtually untranslatable and no one knows quite what it means. There is one reference in Jeremiah 51.56 which is also apocalyptic poetry looking forward to the time when the Persians would come and destroy Babylon which the prophet sees as part of the allowable will of God. In all these four references God does not initiate but allows the wickedness and violence of human actions to work out his own good purposes of salvation for his covenant people.

recompense. It says *"If there is serious injury, you are to take life for life, eye for eye, tooth for tooth, hand for hand, foot for foot, burn for burn, wound for wound, bruise for bruise".* Exodus 21.23-25 [5]

Distributive justice never features in the ministry of the prophets because their primary task was to reveal the nature and purposes of God and they are consistent in revealing the nature of God always linked with salvation, compassion and forgiveness. Of course, there are many times when the prophets have to bring warnings of judgement which they see as the inevitable consequence of spiritual rebellion; of Israel turning away from their covenant responsibilities which were to worship and serve the Lord, and only him.

Judgement follows the breaking of the covenant; but God never breaks his covenant promises. Even though Israel's apostasy many times deserved the full weight of judgement, which would be demanded by standards of distributive justice, God withheld judgement and exercised compassion as demanded by unbreakable love which was the central feature of his nature. The Prophet Hosea beautifully illustrates this when he sees God wrestling with himself , *"How can I give you up, Ephraim? How can I hand you over Israel?... My heart is changed within me; all my compassion is aroused. I will not carry out my fierce anger, nor will I turn and devastate Ephraim. For I am God and not man."*

Hosea 11.8 - 9

Jesus acknowledged that distributive justice was practised in Israel, he said *"You have heard that it was said, 'eye for eye and tooth for tooth.' But I tell you do not resist an evil person"* Matthew 5.38-39. In challenging the regulations given in the Mosaic code Jesus was fully in line with the ministry of the prophets.

The Hebrew concept of God's justice seen through the eyes of the prophets is entirely different because for them 'justice' has a different meaning. It relates to **relationships** rather than legal systems. To be 'just' is to fulfil one's obligations to others. 'Justice' [6] is being faithful to a relationship. When applied to God it means that God is faithful in keeping his covenant promises to act towards his covenant people with unqualified love and generosity. God is acting justly when he fulfils his divine obligations to love

---

[5] Also see Leviticus 24.20 and Deuteronomy 19.21

[6] Hebrew *'tsadaq'*

re-gardless of the cost. In John 3.16 Jesus says that God's love was not just towards Israel but for the world and that it was God's intention not to condemn the world but to save the world through his Son. Paul says that this was always God's intention. He says, *"This grace was given us in Christ Jesus before the beginning of time, but it has now been revealed through the appearing of our Saviour, Christ Jesus, who has destroyed death and has brought life and immortality to light through the gospel".* 2 Timothy 1.9-10

Destroying Death

In Isaiah's final Servant Song, which was a foreshadow of the crucifixion of Jesus, he says that *"by oppression and judgement he was taken away".* The prophet was foreseeing the injustice of the sham trial Jesus was given and that through this he identified with all those who suffer injustice and oppression which was one of the two ways in which people in Isaiah's day thought that God inflicted punishment upon the wicked. The other way was through illness and disease. In this Servant Song it is with utter astonishment that people discover that the one whom they considered *"stricken by God"* was in fact *"crushed for our iniquities".* He actually became one with oppressed and suffering humanity. But although God allowed wicked men to kill his Anointed One, through his death and resurrection the power of death itself was broken and life and immortality was brought to light through the gospel.

This is a mystery which no logical system or rational philosophy can explain. But this is precisely where the Western and the Hebraic mindsets clash. The Hebrew prophets were happy to live with two apparently polar opposites in tension. Hence the prophet can say *"it was the Lord's will to crush him and cause him to suffer"* Isaiah 53.10. This, of course, does not mean that God was directly involved in crushing the Servant and causing him to suffer.

The prophets often do not distinguish between the allowable and the direct will of God. What is being conveyed is that it was **within the purposes** of God for the Servant to suffer. In allowing his Servant to suffer God was acting 'justly' in accordance with his covenant promises and through him he also suffered because part of the divine nature was to suffer with the suffering of his beloved ones. Isaiah 63.9 says, *"In all their distress he too was distressed".* God not only identifies with the suffering of his people but also actually enters into that suffering with them. Thus Paul can say in 2 Corinthians 5.19 (RSV) that *"God was in Christ reconciling the world to himself, not counting their trespasses **against** them, and entrusting to us the message of reconciliation"*.

This Servant Song says, *"By his knowledge my righteous servant will justify many."* Or *"By knowledge of him my righteous Servant will justify many"* Isaiah 53.11 NIV margin. These two different translations show the difficulty of rendering the Hebrew of this verse. Some m/s have *'daath'*, others have *'yada'*. Both mean 'knowledge' although *'yada'* can also be rendered 'humiliation' hence some scholars render this verse as *"By his humiliation my righteous Servant will justify many"*.

Shame was intrinsic to the suffering of the Servant. *"He was assigned a grave with the wicked"* Isaiah 53.9a. But the whole purpose of verses 10 and 11 is to report that God intervenes to vindicate his Servant, to heal him, to revive him and to restore him to new life. Many scholars interpret this as meaning resurrection from the dead, although this is not explicit in the text; but clearly the Lord accomplishes his will through the Servant's suffering. His suffering was vicarious as he *"bore the sin of many"* although he himself was righteous.

People had thought that the Servant, who died childless and in circumstances of extreme suffering and humiliation, was cursed by God. They thought his name was cut off from the land of the living. But God reversed all that and said that, far from being childless, the Servant would *"See his offspring and prolong his days, and the will of the Lord will prosper in his hand"* Isaiah 53.10. He would have children from many nations and his family would go on increasing across the world until the end of time because God had chosen to work out his purposes through his Servant.

The opening line of this Song was that the Servant would be *"raised and lifted up and highly exalted"* and in the final words that theme of exaltation is explained. It is because of what the Servant had done in pouring out his life unto death that God would give him a portion among the great. His inheritance would be among the greatest in world history and his followers the most numerous.

Clearly, there are many similarities between the Servant who willingly endured suffering, humiliation and death and the crucifixion of Jesus. The Servant had taken upon himself the sinfulness of humanity and had been vindicated by God, restored to new life and greatly exalted. Through his death many were brought in to a right (just) relationship with God, a relationship that was a guarantee of life. The fact that it was God himself who was intimately involved in the suffering as well as the exaltation of the Servant is the supreme demonstration of the unbreakable love of God for his people.

Similarly something unique happened in the crucifixion of Jesus that was part of God's eternal plan of salvation for mankind. God's purpose was to release oppressed human beings and to break the power of the forces of darkness that were driving the whole of humanity inevitably towards death - permanent separation from God. At the right time God stepped into human history and did something that the law, given to Israel was unable to do.

Paul describes this graphically in Colossians 2.13 - 14 *"When you were dead in your sins and in the uncircumcision of your sinful nature, God made you alive with Christ. He forgave us all our sins, having cancelled the written code, with its regulations, that was against us and that stood opposed to us; he took it away, nailing it to the cross. And having disarmed the powers and authorities, he made a public spectacle of them, triumphing over them by the cross."*

The Law and Death

For Paul to be able to speak about God cancelling the written code shows the extent to which his Pharisaic training had been left behind when the scales fell from his eyes on the road to Damascus. In his letter to the Galatians he explained that the law was powerless to lead us into a right relationship with God. He said that before faith in Jesus Christ came *"we were held prisoners by the law, locked up until faith should be revealed. So the law was put in charge to lead us to Christ that we might be justified by faith"* Galatians 3.23. The law, of course, was the whole body of teaching given first through Moses and developed by the sages of Judaism over the centuries.

Paul never speaks of parts of the law; in his view the law is the law. You cannot just keep bits of the law, you have to keep the **whole** law and that is not freedom, it is oppression; the law keeps its observants in prison. Looking back upon his life before he found faith in Jesus he saw himself as powerless to achieve a right relationship with God through the law. He said *"I found that the very commandment that was intended to bring life actually brought death"* Romans 7.10. He saw it as a "body of death" from which God, through Jesus Christ, had rescued him [6].

He was able to rejoice that *"If anyone is in Christ, he is a new creation; the old has gone, the new has come!"*   2 Corinthians 5.17

A New Creation

It is this new creation; this new life from death, that is foreseen in Isaiah's great Servant Song that says *"He will see the result of the suffering of his soul and be satisfied"* and that *"by knowledge of him many will be justified"* - that is, brought into a right relationship with God the Father - brought out of death into life. That is the experience of all those who put their faith in Jesus because through his suffering upon the cross he actually accomplished something in the spiritual realm and broke the power of death over sinful humanity. No one can fully explain how this was accomplished but this simply emphasises the fact that we are saved by **faith in Jesus** and not by any other means including the power of our intellect.

Hebraic thinking is perfectly satisfied with the loose ends in our thought processes that this leaves. The prophets of Israel knew that they could never fully search the mind of God. Isaiah actually rejoiced in that fact. He reported God saying to him, *"For my thoughts are not your thoughts, neither are your ways my ways, declares the Lord. As the heavens are higher than the earth, so are my ways higher than your ways and my thoughts than your thoughts".*   Isaiah 55.8 - 9

The Western mind by contrast attempts to reduce everything to systems. We process everything into a logical framework including our knowledge of God. But in so doing we distort the truth and reduce God to a size that we can cope with in our limited understanding. But the God of Western theology is not the God of the Bible. All too often he is a puny little construction of our Western culture moulded either in the liberal tradition or the evangelical.

Admittedly this statement does scant justice to the dedicated service of countless liberals and evangelicals but it makes the point that when we fail to grasp the concept of God as revealed

---

[6] See Romans 7.24

through the prophets which forms the background to the whole of the New Testament - the Gospels and the writings of the Apostles - we are in grave danger of failing to understand the nature and purposes of God.

Nowhere is this more apparent than in our Western understanding of this fourth Servant Song and its relation to the cross of Christ our Saviour. The central statement is *"The punishment that brought us peace was upon him, and by his wounds we are healed."* Isaiah 53.5. The equivalent statement in Paul's writings is found in Romans Chapter 5. The opening verse says, *"Therefore, since we have been justified through faith, we have peace with God through our Lord Jesus Christ, through whom we have gained access by faith into this grace in which we now stand."*

Justice in Hebraic Context

Paul is referring to the new relationship with God that has been established by faith in Jesus for all believers. This new relationship enables us to experience an outpouring of the love of God into our hearts by the Holy Spirit Romans 5.5. The term he uses *"God has poured out his love"* is the same as that used in Acts 10.45 where the Holy Spirit is said to have been *"poured out"* onto the Gentiles. He then engages in a type of rabbinic argument much of the point of which is lost in many English translations due to the mistranslation of the words *'dikaios'* and *'dikaiosune'* as 'righteous' and 'righteousness' instead of 'just' and 'justice'.

The whole of Romans Chapter 5 takes on a new meaning when it is read in an Hebraic context instead of a product of Western culture as in most English translations. It is a useful exercise in getting an understanding of Paul's theology to sit down and read right through Romans in any English translation and each time you read the word 'righteous' or 'righteousness', substitute 'just' or 'justice'.

The NIV translation of Romans 5.7 fails to bring out the contrast Paul intends. It says, *"Very rarely will anyone die for a righteous man, though for a good man someone might possibly dare to die"*. But the Greek says, *"Very rarely will anyone die for a **just** man, though for a **virtuous** man someone might possibly dare to die"*. The **just** man was one who was in right relationships with other people and was upright in all his dealings (though not necessarily warm-hearted) whereas the **virtuous** man was one who actively did good deeds to other people.

Paul then refers[7] to the way God demonstrates his love by Christ dying for us while we were still sinners - when we had nothing to commend ourselves and were actually hostile towards God.

But we have been 'justified' - brought into a right relationship with God - through the blood of Christ which saves us from wrath. The Greek does not use the word "God". It simply refers to "the wrath"[8] rather than "the wrath of God", although Paul does not hesitate to use the phrase *"the wrath of God"* in other contexts such as in Romans 1.18, *"The wrath of God is being revealed from heaven against all the godlessness and wickedness of men who suppress the truth by their wickedness..."*

Justification

In Romans Chapter 5 Paul is referring to the general condition of humanity, separated from God since the time of Adam. The reason is that Adam deliberately disobeyed a commandment of God, which resulted in all human beings being separated from God. What Jesus has done through the cross is to break the power of that spiritual death (separation from God) to which all are condemned and made it possible for all human beings to enter a new and living relationship with God the Creator.

Through the death and resurrection of Christ it is possible to receive God's abundant provision of grace and the gift of justification - being brought into a right relationship with God so that his love is poured into our lives - and we move from the realm of darkness and death into the realm of light and life.

Paul's rabbinic argument sees the sinfulness of all humankind stemming from Adam but being intensified for the people of Israel through the giving of the teaching at Sinai because this enabled the covenant people of God to know the requirements of God, so when they broke those requirements they were doing so **wilfully** and in the knowledge of right and wrong. This was the charge against the nation brought by Jeremiah when he was told to go up and down the streets of Jerusalem and search for one person who was dealing honestly and seeking the truth. He went first to the ordinary people and then to the leaders saying *"Surely they*

---

[7] Romans 5.6 - 8

[8] Romans 5.9

know the way of the Lord, the requirements of their God".

He found that they had all *"with one accord"* broken the covenant relationship with God Jeremiah 5.1-5. There was no excuse. They could not plead ignorance of the word of God which they had had since the time of Moses.

The rest of mankind sinned in ignorance because they only had their conscience to guide them. But now, through Messiah Jesus, everyone had the opportunity of coming into a right relationship with God through what Jesus had achieved on the cross in breaking the power of darkness and death. But this has not automatically brought everyone into a right relationship with God. Each individual has to accept the 'justification' offered through the gospel. He says that through the obedience of the 'Righteous One' justification is available to the many [8].

The difficulty we face in understanding this is because we simply do not think in the framework of the prophets of Israel whose whole worldview was formed by the presence of God and the belief that everything that happened was either his 'direct will' or his 'allowable will'. In the fourth Servant Song Isaiah was foreseeing a time coming when God would precipitate a confrontation with the powers of darkness and death which were holding humanity in a state of oppression and separation from himself. He believed that God had allowed the Exile to take place in order to break the hold that idolatry had over his covenant people; that the misery of exile from the beloved City of Jerusalem and the oppression of slavery would cause them to cry out to him, the God of their fathers, for help.

A Light for the Gentiles

They would then realise that God was not simply a territorial God only to be found in the land of Israel, but he was omnipresent and omnipotent; he held the nations in his hands as *'a drop in a bucket'* and brought the most powerful kings and rulers of great empires to nothing. Isaiah knew that it was God's intention to bring his redeemed people back to the land of their fathers, forgiven and cleansed from the sins that caused the Exile. They were to be a light for the Gentiles to radiate God's presence to the surrounding nations; to carry the revelation of his truth to all peoples so that

---

[8] See Romans 5.19

everyone would have the opportunity of knowing him and coming into a right relationship with the eternal God Creator of the universe.

The Servant of the Lord

The first Servant Song [9] radiated this confidence in the mission of Israel as the Servant of the Lord, *"Here is my servant whom I uphold, my chosen one in whom I delight; I will put my Spirit on him and he will bring justice to the nations"* Isaiah 42.1. The second part of the first Servant Song [10] carries the same confidence, *This is what God the Lord says - he who created the heavens and stretched them out, who spread out the earth and all that comes out of it, who gives breath to its people, and life to those who walk on it... I will keep you and make you to be a covenant for the people and a light for the Gentiles..."*

By the time we reach the fourth Servant Song that confidence in the nation as the obedient servant of the Lord has gone. It has been replaced by the recognition that the messianic mission of Israel will be accomplished by *an individual* rather than the nation as a whole. It recognises that God would achieve his purposes in a way that turns upside down the values of the world.

His Servant would achieve the breaking of the powers of darkness and death that enslave the whole of mankind, not through political power, or military might, or any other form of human ability. He would achieve the purposes of God through humility and

---

[9] The four Servant Songs in Isaiah fall into seven parts. They are, 42.1 - 4 and 5 - 9; 49.1 - 6 and 7 - 13; 50.4 - 9 and 10 - 11; 52.13 - 53.12. Each of the first three songs has three themes.

The first song sets out the key objectives of the Servant whose task is (1) to bring justice to the nations; (2) to bring justice in truth; (3) to establish justice on the whole earth. Verses 1 – 4 set out the way he will not do this by the usual human exercise of power.

The Second Song has three themes which have close parallels with Jeremiah. (1) the election of the Servant, his call and equipment, see Jeremiah 1.5; (2) his despondency, see Jeremiah 15.10-18 and 20.7-18; (3) his new task – to bring light for the Gentile nations.

The Third Song also has three themes which have close parallels with Jeremiah and the Gospels. (1) the means by which the Servant receives his instruction, see Jeremiah 15.16 and 18.20, and John 12.49; (2) the acceptance of the inevitability of opposition and suffering, see Jeremiah 11.19, 20.8 and 18, and Matthew 16.21; (3) the response to the Servant (those who are patient and trust the Lord will receive the light. Those who are impatient generate their own light and come to a bad end)

[10] Isaiah 42. 5 - 9

suffering; through being utterly despised and rejected by the proud and lofty. He would suffer a most terrible form of death at the hands of sinful and cruel humanity, but in so doing he would identify with sinful humanity and he would break open a new and living way in which, by faith, all could enter.

The Way to Life

In order to enter this new relationship with God human beings would have to leave behind their worldly values moulded by wealth, by intellect, by status and the desire for human adulation. They would have to become like little children trusting their Father and simply be prepared to leave behind all that the great civilisations of humanity had taught them. They would have to accept that breaking the power of sin that was driving them inexorably towards death was something they could not do for themselves. In that very act of self-renunciation and recognition of human helplessness would come salvation. It would come through an acceptance of the mission of Messiah and through faith in him.

Isaiah recognised that this was the way to life; to be justified, to be brought into a right relationship with God who would pour out his love over the penitent sinner. As God would transform the marred figure of the Servant, in the same way he would transform all those who were identified with him. They would leave behind the old humanity that leads to death and become a new creation that leads to life everlasting.

Western Christians who are rich in the things of this world and whose thinking is moulded by Western civilisation are like the rich man whom Jesus told that he would find it very difficult to enter the Kingdom.[11] In Romans 12.2 Paul warns the Roman believers against allowing the secular world to determine their social values. J B Phillips' translation is probably the closest to capturing the essence of what Paul was saying in this definitive statement. *"Don't let the world around you squeeze you into its own mould, but let God re-mould your minds from within, so that you may prove in practice that the Plan of God for you is good, meets all His demands and moves towards the goal of true maturity."*

---

[11] See Mark 10.17 - 27

Distorted Theology

We have lost the community and corporate thinking that was the background to the world of the prophets of ancient Israel and of the Apostle Paul and the Hebraic writers of the New Testament. We have individualised our concept of society. This has even distorted our understanding of God's greatest act of redemption through the cross of Christ. We have made it into an act of individual atonement that has distorted the nature of God, which he revealed through the prophets of ancient Israel.

The prophets showed God as a God of love and forgiveness. We have made him an unforgiving tyrant demanding full satisfaction. Our Western theology, based upon distributive justice, demands that everyone gets exactly what they deserve and we do not realise how this distorts the nature of God.

Just think of this: A is owed a large sum of money by B and A demands that it is paid in full, but B cannot pay. Then along comes C and pays the debt to A so that B is now free of debt. But A has not really forgiven B; he has had the debt repaid, but he has not forgiven the debtor. He has merely had his demands satisfied by a third-party. This is not the nature of God as revealed in the prophets of Israel or in the teaching of Jesus in the New Testament - a God who demands full satisfaction before he will offer forgiveness.

This kind of theology is present in a lot of modern songs. Some have memorable tunes that make them favourites such as **"In Christ alone"** which has the words –

"Till on that cross as Jesus died,

The wrath of God was satisfied,

For every sin on him was laid,

Here in the death of Christ I live." [12]

This kind of modern Western theology diminishes the crucifixion of Christ. It reduces Jesus' death on the cross to an act of atonement for our individual sins. This misses the point of the mighty act of God's salvation, which was to break the curse of death hanging over the whole of mankind. When the Temple

---

[12] I personally think this is a beautiful song and I love singing it in worship, but I cannot sing this particular verse with its unbiblical theology.

curtain was torn asunder as Jesus died upon the cross, the veil of separation between humanity and the One True Holy God the Creator of the Universe was also torn asunder. It is difficult for our finite human minds to comprehend the significance of this momentous act of redemption in which God himself intervened in the course of human history to open up the way to himself that had so far only been found by a small minority of spiritual giants in the tiny covenant nation of Israel.

Influence of the Enlightenment

Western teachers who like to reduce all complex concepts into rational thought systems cannot cope with the untidy Hebraic practice of leaving unresolved concepts which often appear to be contradictory. The Hebrew prophets knew that they could never fully understand the mind of God or systematise his ways in the natural order of creation or his dealings with humanity. They were content to leave many unknowns as incomprehensible; but this is unsatisfactory to the modern Western scholar and our theologians have been strongly influenced by the kind of rationalism that is the outcome of the Enlightenment.

Evangelicals often do not realise the extent to which they too have been influenced by the Enlightenment especially in their individualistic interpretation of sin and salvation. This is reflected in many of the modern songs that are popular in evangelical worship. They may have nice tunes that we like to sing but they are not biblical theology and they distort our image of God.

Too many Christians today are learning their understanding of God from the songs they sing rather than from the Bible. There are serious consequences if our knowledge of the nature of God is not based upon biblical revelation. It means that we are unable to be faithful witnesses, revealing the word of God to a hungry world, where there is a desperate need to know the true nature of God who goes to any lengths to save his people from death.

Common Identity of Believers

Western society has largely lost the sense of 'corporate identity' that pervaded the world of the Hebrew prophets. In our highly individualised social context we have lost the way God deals with communities diminishing our understanding of the 'community of believers' established by Jesus which is the Church of the New Testament - the 'company of the redeemed' who were the first born of the Kingdom. They were described by Peter as, *"A chosen people, a royal priesthood, a holy nation, a people belonging to God, that you may declare the praises of him who called you out of darkness into his wonderful light"* 1 Peter 2.9. In the next verse Peter makes a highly significant sociological statement, *"Once you were not a people, but now you are the people of God."*

The New Testament church was a body of people - Jews and Gentiles, Greeks and Romans, Asians and Europeans, young and old, male and female, rich and poor, slaves and aristocrats - who had no common identity other than that they were believers in Jesus and through him they had entered into a new dimension of life, a living relationship with God.

Formerly they had not been a 'community' in any valid sociological sense of that word, but through Christ they had become a community - recognising a common belongingness - brought together by their love for God and for one another, as a response to the love they had received through Jesus.

They had experienced the love and forgiveness of God revealed through his One and only Son. This created a tremendously powerful sense of common identity. They belonged to one another because they belonged to God. They belonged to God because they belonged to Jesus and were part of his company of disciples.

In our advanced Western individualism we have lost a precious element of the gospel - an understanding of the nature of God as Father. This has resulted in a society in which both community and family life are fragmented. Western society today is starved of fatherhood. Millions of children have no personal knowledge of the love of a father and until we recover a biblical understanding of the nature of God this basic concept will continue to be lost.

This is what Jesus both taught and revealed - that the Father has no favourites; that he loves each one of his children and loves them so much that he longs for them to be in full communion with him and in an intimate relationship of 'sonship' with him. In order to achieve this he had to reveal the depth of his love and forgiveness which he did through allowing Jesus freely to choose to go through the crucifixion.

When we come into a biblical understanding of the love and forgiveness of God in line with the revelation given to the prophets, we realise that we are not simply saved for ourselves but we are 'saved to serve' and we are part of a serving community - the servant of God. We then identify with all members of the worldwide body of believers, so we identify with persecuted Christians in societies far removed from our Western privileged nations because we are part of the same family. Without this understanding of the love and forgiveness of God we can never understand or experience what it is to be part of the family of God which was at the heart, not only of the New Testament body of believers, but also of the nation of Israel under the old covenant.

God of Love and Forgiveness

From earliest times God had revealed his love and forgiveness to those who were seeking to know him. Moses had clearly grasped an understanding of the nature of God when he faced a full-scale rebellion of the nation soon after their release from slavery in Egypt. He had sent a reconnaissance party into Canaan and they came back saying that it was indeed a fertile land but the people were too strong for them. Moses' leadership was challenged and the people even contemplated returning to Egypt.

This was not just rebellion against Moses, it was rebellion against God through a lack of trust in the Lord, but Moses pleaded with God not to allow them to die in the desert. He knew that *"The Lord is slow to anger, abounding in love and forgiving sin and rebellion,"* so he pleaded with God, *"In accordance with your great love, forgive the sin of these people, just as you have pardoned them from the time they left Egypt until now."* Numbers 14.18 - 19

The whole nation of Israel knew that God was a God of love and forgiveness. This is mentioned many times in the Psalms such as, *"You are forgiving and good, O Lord, abounding in love to all who call to you"* Psalm 86.5. Many times the Psalmist rejoices in this forgiveness. *"Blessed is he whose transgressions are forgiven, whose sins are covered. Blessed is the man whose sins the Lord does not count against him."* Psalm 32.1 - 2

It was an essential part of the message of the prophets to speak about the love and forgiveness of God. Jeremiah's great prophecy of the New Covenant included the promise from God, *"I will forgive their wickedness and remember their sins no more"* Jeremiah 31.34 and the solemn promise that God gave to Solomon at the dedication of the temple was a promise of forgiveness, *"If my people, who are called by my name, will humble themselves and pray and seek my face and turn from their wicked ways, then I will hear from heaven and will forgive their sin and will heal their land".*   2 Chronicles 7.14

This promise of forgiveness given to Israel was extended to all nations through a promise God gave to Jeremiah, *"If at any time I announce that a nation or kingdom is to be uprooted, torn down and destroyed, and that nation I warned repents of it evil, then I will relent and not inflict on it the disaster I had planned."*
                                                                        Jeremiah 18.7 - 8

This understanding of the love and forgiveness of God is carried over into the New Testament where it is a major element in the teaching of Jesus who said to his disciples, *"If you will forgive men when they sin against you, your heavenly Father will also forgive you".*   Matthew 6.14

That 'full and complete forgiveness' is made possible to all who have faith in Jesus through his crucifixion and resurrection. Paul describes the power of the cross to break the powers of evil that separate humans from God, *"having disarmed the powers and authorities, he made a public spectacle of them, triumphing over them by the cross"* Colossians 2.15. This was Paul's understanding of the significance of the fourth Servant Song where the Servant *"poured out his life unto death and was numbered with the transgressors".*   Isaiah 53.12

The atoning death of Messiah Jesus was much more than the mere forgiving of our individual sins as Western individualised theology portrays. It was a once and for all-time action in which God conquered the power of death *"through the appearing of Christ Jesus who destroyed death and has brought life and immortality to light through the gospel."* [13] The cross has made it possible for all humanity to come into a new and living relationship with God through the resurrection of Jesus. It overcame the spiritual separation of humanity from God that has existed since Adam.

---

[13] See 2 Timothy 1.10

[14] This is the theme developed by Paul in 1 Corinthians 15.
See particularly 15.45 - 49

Through the first Adam came death but through the second Adam came life. [14] This is why Jesus was able to assert with divine authority that no one comes to the Father except through him.

He is indeed the Way, the Truth and the Life for all who put their trust in him.

Chapter Ten

GOD'S FATHERLY LOVE

This chapter traces the Hebraic roots of the 'Fatherhood of God' which is central to the New Testament and the teaching of Jesus. It shows the reason why God is not referred to as Father in the Old Testament until after the return from exile in Babylon.

The Fatherhood of God hardly features in the Old Testament although it is central to the message of the New Testament. In this chapter we want to explore the Hebraic roots of the Fatherhood of God which paved the way for the unique revelation which Jesus brought to our understanding of 'fatherhood' and the love of God as our Father. This was of supreme importance in the mission of Jesus and in the teaching he gave, both in private and in his public ministry.

Jesus taught his disciples to honour the name of God as *"Our Father in heaven"* Matthew 6.9. He gave them a practical example of the Father's love, *"As the Father has loved me, so have I loved you"* John 15.9. He spoke of the Fatherly love of God for them, *The Father himself loves you because you have loved me"* John 16.27. And he prayed to the Father for his disciples, *"Holy Father protect them by the power of your name"* John 17.11. Similarly, throughout the Epistles there are numerous references to God as Father. Paul even uses the familiar Hebraic term, *"Abba Father"* Romans 8.15. So where are the Hebraic roots of the Fatherhood of God and why was there such reluctance to refer to God as 'Father' among the prophets and in the early history of Israel?

Prior to the exile, all the prophets had to deal with outbreaks of idolatry in the nation. They were always strong in their condemnation of idolatrous practices which were seen as evidence of unfaithfulness to God and as breaking the covenant relationship that had been established by God. A central part of that covenant was that Israel would acknowledge no other God. Yahweh was their God and they would serve no other. To turn to other gods was rebellion against God.

During their time in Egypt the Israelites were no doubt exposed to the worship of Egyptian gods and by the end of the Exile many would have forgotten the God of their fathers Abraham, Isaac and Jacob. When Moses was called to go and tell the people that God was calling them to come out of Egypt he protested that the people would not even know the name of God[1]. He himself had to be taught that name. Even when the tribes were in the wilderness, separated from the influence of other nations, they were unfaithful. They made a golden calf and invented their own idolatrous religion which was severely dealt with by Moses.

Canaanite Influence

But the real test of their covenant loyalty came after the settlement in Canaan. All the surrounding Gentile nations and communities had their own gods who could be seen; unlike Israel's unseen God whom they could not even describe to their Canaanite neighbours. The local gods were usually regarded as territorial with jurisdiction over the land as well as its people which often resulted in fertility cults to induce greater productivity from the soil.

The newly settled Israelite tribes had no experience of arable farming which they had to learn from the local people who also taught them about the local gods. Cultic sexual practices were often linked with the worship of the local Baal and these were attractive to the Israelite men but they were abhorrent to the prophets of Israel. The Canaanite local gods were often worshipped as sons of the national god El at various high places, and these practices were fiercely resisted by the prophets of Israel.

This is the reason why references to God as Father are sparse throughout the Old Testament. The earliest references are found in Deuteronomy 32.6 in what is known as the 'Song of Moses' where the question is asked, *"Is he not your Father, your Creator, who made you and formed you?"* The Hebrew is somewhat uncertain here but even if we accept the NIV translation of, *"your Creator"*, rather than *"who bought you"*[2], the question clearly refers to the origins of the nation rather than to the nature of God as Father. Additionally, other references, such as Psalm 89.26 and Malachi 2.10 have a similar connotation of God choosing the

---

[1] Exodus 3.13

[2] NIV margin

offspring of Abraham as his covenant people through whom he would work out his purposes. In that sense he created, or physically 'fathered' the nation.

Fatherhood in Hosea

The first references in the writing prophets to the nature of God as Father are to be found in the eighth century prophet Hosea. He was the first prophet who dared to speak of God in terms of Fatherhood although he did so in veiled, rather than direct terms. His ministry was examined in Chapter Three where we noted that Hosea's own experience of love, marriage and family, probably had a bearing on his understanding of God. Hosea's description of the divine dilemma concerning whether or not to enforce judgement upon the rebellious nation of Israel is a spiritual gem.

There are few other passages in the Bible that get closer to the heart of God than his description of God arguing with himself, *"My heart is changed within me; all my compassion is aroused. I will not carry out my fierce anger ... for I am God and not man"* Hosea 11.8-9. This clearly reveals a father's heart over a wayward child and it is an enormous leap forward in revelation for the prophet to apply this to God and his relationship with Israel as his covenant people. He follows this in the next verse with a reference to God's children coming to him which is further evidence that Hosea saw God as the Father of the nation.

Two chapters later Hosea records God grieving over his people as he recalls how he brought them out of Egypt and cared for them in the desert. But, *"when I fed them, they were satisfied; when they were satisfied, they became proud; then they forgot me"* Hosea 13.4-6. Those final words, *"then they forgot me"* express the grieving heart of the Father who had done everything possible for his children and they still turned their backs upon him. It is an amazing revelation of God that came out of the prophet's own personal experience of broken love and his grief as he saw the nation he loved turning away from God and facing catastrophic destruction at the hands of the Assyrians. Hosea knew that this was a tragedy that would not have happened if the people had been faithful to the Lord because his protection would have been over them.

Jeremiah is the first of the writing prophets of Israel to speak of God directly as Father which provides one of the many parallels with the ministry of Jesus. There are three such references. They are in 3.4, 3.19 and 31.9. They all deal with the same theme - the future reuniting of the scattered tribes of Israel and Judah. This is highly significant in understanding the new and unique revelation that was given to the prophet Jeremiah and which provides yet another link with the ministry of Jesus.

Jeremiah was deeply concerned, from the earliest days of his ministry during the reign of Josiah, with the fate of the northern kingdom of Israel that had been absorbed into the Assyrian Empire 100 years earlier. He longed to see the tribes reunited and coming up to Jerusalem together to seek the Lord without all the trappings of religion, such as the Ark of the Covenant[3], but coming purely out of a love for God; a desire to seek him and to worship him.

In 3:17 Jeremiah foresees a time coming when not only Judah and Israel, but all nations will gather in Jerusalem to honour the name of the Lord. He foresees the returning exiles from Judah and Israel coming from 'a northern land' which usually refers to either Nineveh or Babylon - in this case to both. He foresees Jerusalem becoming the centre of worship for people of all nations and they will call the city *'The Throne of the Lord'*.

The whole of this passage, 3.14 - 18, is a call to the people of both Judah and Israel to return to the Lord. Jeremiah was foreseeing God using the tragedy of exile to forge a new unity among his covenant people and in due time he would bring them back to the land and use them to gather all nations to worship God. This may be a forerunner for Isaiah's vision of the redeemed people of Israel returning to the land and being a *'light for the Gentiles'*. Isaiah 49.6

This same theme of national unity overcoming tribal differences is played out in chapter 31[4] where Jeremiah foresees the time when all the tribes of Israel will return to the Lord as one people. He

---

[3] See Jeremiah 3.16 which is the last reference to the Ark of the Covenant in the history of Israel and may indicate that the Ark had already been removed by the Babylonians when they took the first wave of prisoners into slavery after the surrender of Jerusalem in 596 BC. It is also possible that the Ark had been hidden before the arrival of the Babylonians as there is no reference to it in Babylonian records as the spoils of war. Some archaeologists believe that the Ark was hidden under the Holy of Holies and may still be there alongside the ruins of the Western walls in Jerusalem. But the Ark was not important to Jeremiah. He looked forward to the day when people will not grieve for the Ark but will seek God with a pure heart.

[4] referred to in Chapter Seven 'Love Changes a Nation'

sees them coming from 'the land of the North'[5] and gathering from the ends of the earth. He sees the blind and the lame and expectant mothers among them, all weeping and praying as they return to Zion. He could see God leading them beside streams of water and on a level path so that no one would stumble, *"because I am Israel's Father, and Ephraim is my firstborn son".*

Jeremiah 31.9

This is a beautiful picture of the fatherly love of God for his people and Jeremiah was the first to be given such a revelation. It is significant that this understanding of the nature of God was born out of the tragedy of the destruction of Jerusalem and the period of exile in Babylon. It was out of the suffering and bitterness of judgement which the nation had brought upon itself that this new understanding of the nature and purposes of God was born.

Progressive Revelation

In receiving this revelation Jeremiah was foreseeing events more than fifty years beyond his lifetime. But there is another reference in the Old Testament that comes from the period that Jeremiah was prophetically describing. It is to be found in the last part of Isaiah where there are three references to God as "Father" which are of great significance. They add to the revelation first given to Hosea, then developed by Jeremiah, and in Isaiah become a full declaration of Fatherhood. The height of revelation is reached in the prophetic announcement, *"You are our Father".*

We need to look at this assertion in context. The words are in Isaiah 63.8 - 10 and 16.

*"He said, surely they are my people, sons who will not be false to me; and so he became their Saviour. In all their distress he too was distressed, and the angel of his presence saved them. In his love and mercy he redeemed them; he lifted them up and carried them all the days of old. Yet they have rebelled and grieved his Holy Spirit. So he turned and became their enemy and he himself fought against them...**But you are our Father,** though Abraham does not know us or Israel acknowledge us; you, O Lord, **are our Father**, our Redeemer from of old is your name."*

This is the only place in the Old Testament where the words,

---

[5] See Jeremiah 31.8

"You are our Father" occur. The writing prophets of Israel were all hesitant in referring to God as a Father or in speaking of themselves as sons of God. The earlier prophets would have said that they were not God's sons, they were his creatures. He had created men and women in his own image, but they were not gods or sons of the gods as in Gentile religions. In the minds of the prophets there was a clear distinction. They could not allow people to think of Yahweh, the God of Israel, in the same way as the gods of the Gentiles.

But gradually God took them beyond their spiritual infancy to the point where they could receive the full revelation of his Fatherhood that would reach the height of revelation in the ministry and teaching of Jesus. This is a wonderful example of God's progressive revelation of his nature and purposes given through the prophets of Israel. That revelation was born in a crucible of suffering as Hosea foresaw the approaching catastrophe that would destroy the northern kingdom of of Israel which he was powerless to prevent - a tragedy to which he was sensitised by his own personal suffering.

That revelation was developed in somewhat similar circumstances through Jeremiah's 40 years of unheeded warnings of the destruction of Jerusalem. His anguish and personal suffering are seen on every page of the Book that bears his name. Finally, after the exile in Babylon, the suffering of those who returned to the desolate city of Jerusalem prepared them for the revelation of the loving Father who welcomed the prodigal sons back to the land he had given them long ago. They were now ready to realise that he had been with him all along, entering into their sufferings and longing for them to come back from the far country to be embraced by his Fatherly love.

Fatherhood in Isaiah

This passage from Isaiah 63.7 to 64.12 is of unique value in that it represents a milestone in the spiritual development of the Hebraic understanding of the nature of God. Three times the prophet uses the phrase *"O Lord, you are our Father"* Isaiah 63.16 and 64.8. The passage is a 'song of lament', bewailing the distressed state of the nation, recognising and confessing the sinfulness of the people that has brought them to this sorry state; recognising also their utter dependence upon their Lord and Saviour and calling upon him to save them. *"All of us have become like one who is unclean, and all our righteous acts are like filthy rags; we all shrivel up like a leaf, and like the wind our sins sweep us away".*

Isaiah 64.6

The song comes from the early days of the post-exilic period when the first settlers were back in the land viewing the desolation of Jerusalem with dismay and wondering how they will ever get the strength to rebuild the nation and even to provide basic food and shelter for their families. It can be dated some time between the arrival of the first returnees in 537 BC and the beginning of the rebuilding of the temple under Haggai in 520 BC. Enthusiasm following the release from Babylon had given way to despondency and despair at the desolation all around them. Yet we have here an amazing statement of faith.

The unique revelation that is here, and nowhere else in the Old Testament, is that God is the true Father of the nation. He is not like Abraham or Israel who are both dead and cannot acknowledge them [6]. He is the one who redeemed them long ago and in the recent past. He is the one who has watched over them through all the different circumstances of their history. Now they have arrived back in Jerusalem, utterly exhausted and totally dismayed at what they have found. Their only hope is in God. Suddenly, in their helplessness, they realised how much God has loved them and that he is in fact their true Father.

The song celebrates God's saving act in history of how he came to rescue them when they were distressed in Egypt. *"In his love and mercy he redeemed them; he lifted them up and carried them all the days of old."* Jeremiah 63.9. They further recalled the days of their forefathers in the days of Moses whom God led as a shepherd his flock and guided them by his Holy Spirit. When they wandered from the way of the Lord, enemies overran the land, *"They rebelled and grieved his Holy Spirit. So he turned and became their enemy"* Isaiah 63.10 but now they were back in the land where all the cities, including Jerusalem, were a desolation.

Even the temple where their fathers used to praise the Lord had been burned with fire. They recognised that all the people had become unclean before God yet they knew of his love and mercy. He had released them from the oppression of Babylon

---

[6] See Isaiah 63.16

and they now recognised his great love for them as a Father loves his children even when they are wayward.

This is probably the most powerful psalm of communal lamentation in the Bible showing the ebbs and flows of history and testifying to the vital power of God and his incomparable goodness and awe-inspiring holiness. The psalm is a conver-sation with the Lord remembering the tenderness and compassion with which the Spirit of the Lord guided his people as they left the oppressors behind in Babylon and made their way towards the land of their fathers. They called out to the Lord to *"look down from heaven and see from your lofty throne, holy and glorious"*.   Isaiah 63.15

They confessed their sinfulness but nevertheless cried out to God *"Yet, Lord, you are our Father. We are the clay, you are the Potter; we are all the work of your hand. Do not be angry beyond measure, O Lord; do not remember our sins for ever."* Isaiah 64.8-9

Highpoint of Revelation

The high point in revelation was reached through the recognition of the amazing patience of God who, like a father watching over his rebellious children, had watched over Israel since the birth of the nation. It was he, in fact, who had actually birthed the nation and called them into a covenant relationship with himself. Despite all their sinfulness he still loved them and watched over them. He was indeed their true Father in Heaven.

This is the highest point of revelation in the Old Testament of the Fatherhood of God. It was a daring declaration by the prophet. But it could not have happened before the exile. All the earlier prophets of Israel had chastised the nation for falling into idolatry but after the exile there is no further mention of idolatry. If there's one thing that the exile achieved it is the breaking of the power of idolatry. It may be that the people saw so much of the horrors of idolatry in Babylon that it spiritually immunised them from future temptation. So now, those who came back to the land of Judah were a spiritually redeemed remnant who could receive the final revelation of the nature of God through the prophets of Israel - his Fatherhood. This paved the way for the revelation of Jesus who devoted so much of his ministry to teaching his disciples about the Fatherhood of God.

This Chapter would be incomplete without looking briefly at the full development of the revelation of the Fatherhood of God in the ministry of Jesus for which the prophets of Israel prepared the way. Indeed, it is our view that the ministry and teaching of Jesus can only be understood within the foundational context of the revelation given by God to those prophets.

As the writer to the Hebrews says,

"In the past God spoke to our forefathers through the prophets at many times and in various ways, but in these last days he has spoken to us by his Son, whom he appointed heir of all things, and through whom he made the universe. The Son is the radiance of God's glory and the exact representation of his being, sustaining all things by his powerful word. After he had provided purification for sins, he sat down at the right hand of the Majesty in heaven." Hebrews 1.1 - 3

The Incarnation

This prologue to the Book of Hebrews provides a bridge between the prophets of ancient Israel who ministered under the Old Covenant and the disciples of Jesus who were apostles of the New Covenant. It emphasises the continuity in God's self-revelation beginning with the patriarchs and the prophets and culminating in the incarnation of Jesus. There is an obvious link here with the prologue in the Fourth Gospel where Jesus is described as the 'Word of God' through whom the whole universe was created. He was the 'Word made flesh', the 'exact representation' of God and the fulfilment of the promise God had given to the prophets many generations earlier.

The testimony of the Gospels and the New Testament writers is perfectly clear in expressing the belief that Jesus was actually the incarnation of God. This was Jesus' own testimony when the religious authorities had moved into the next stage in testing his claims to be Messiah and were putting direct questions to him. In John 10.22f there is a record of Jesus walking in the temple area when they asked him, *"How long will you keep us in suspense? If you are the Messiah, tell us plainly."* Part of Jesus' response was the definitive statement, *"I and the Father are one"*.John 10.30

This was central to the teaching that Jesus gave to his own disciples. When they were staying in the region of the springs of the River Jordan, popularly known as Caesarea Philippi, they discussed his Messianic mission. '*"But what about you?"* he asked, *"Who do you say I am?"* Simon Peter answered, *"You are the Messiah, the Son of the living God".*   Matthew 16.15 - 16

It is interesting to note that immediately after this incident Matthew records *"From that time on Jesus began to explain to his disciples that he must go to Jerusalem and suffer many things at the hands of the elders, chief priests and teachers of the law, and that he must be killed and on the third day be raised to life".* Matthew 16.21

Clearly, Jesus was already identifying with the Messiah of Isaiah 53 rather than that of Isaiah 16. In his teaching of the disciples he emphasised the close relationship between himself and the Father. He told Thomas that if he really knew him he would also know the Father. He stated this explicitly, *"Anyone who has seen me has seen the Father"* John 14.9. It is this claim to divinity that led directly to the crucifixion.

For those who accept the testimony of Jesus and that of the eyewitnesses recorded in the New Testament, this relationship with God the Father is of the greatest significance in evaluating his actions and his teaching. It transforms what would otherwise be the wise words of an outstanding teacher into an actual revelation of God. That is the significance of the incarnation. Once we accept that Jesus is the incarnation of God his words and deeds can be measured alongside the revelation given to the prophets under the Old Covenant and may be seen as the full and final revelation of God.

Love and Compassion

In Jesus we see the embodiment of love, forgiveness and compassion both in his teaching and in his life. Jesus acted both in line with the teaching of the prophets and also added to the revelation they were given. This, of course, is exactly what we would expect from a full and final revelation of God through his Messiah. In his treatment of women we see something of Jesus' tenderness. The woman caught in adultery was not condemned to be stoned in accordance with the law, but was advised to go away and change her lifestyle. Similarly, the woman at the well in Samaria who was living with a man not her husband was not condemned but treated with respect and taught something of the nature of God and true worship.

Jesus also showed love and compassion in many different

circumstances and with people in different ranks of society such as the blind, beggars, and even prostitutes and lepers who were among the outcasts of society. He wept at the graveside of his friend Lazarus when he grieved at the unbelief of even his close friends. He wept again during the final week of his life as he looked at the City of Jerusalem from the Mount of Olives foreseeing what was coming to the City and to the covenant people of God who were rejecting the Messiah whom God had sent.

Jesus was probably not only foreseeing the slaughter of half a million people in Judah at the hands of the Romans but also the 2,000 year Diaspora culminating in the Central European Holocaust of the 20th century. This grief was all part of Jesus' love and compassion for the lost sheep of Israel and was a reflection of the very heart of God.

The Command to Love

It is in the teaching that Jesus gave to his disciples that we probably come closest to the heart of God and see the clearest revelation of the Father's love and of his desire for right relationships with his children and between each of his children. Central to his teaching was Jesus' command to the disciples to love each other. This was not a mild request or an optional extra, but a **command** to be obeyed. Thus loving relationships were central to discipleship and an essential element at the heart of the kingdom community.

The Fourth Gospel majors on this part of Jesus' teaching. It was after supper during the last week when Jesus had washed his disciples' feet that he began to stress the importance of love. He said *"A new command I give you: Love one another. As I have loved you, so you must love one another. By this all men will know that you are my disciples, if you love one another"*.   John 13.34

This expression of love in the communal life of the disciples was related to the love of the Father in Jesus' teaching. In a conversation with the disciples, recorded in John 14.21, Jesus said *"whoever has my commands and obeys them, he is the one who loves me. He who loves me will be loved by my Father, and I too will love him and show myself to him."* This is a definitive statement that gets to the heart of relationships with God the Father.

Those who have a relationship of love with Jesus will be loved by the Father and will also be in communication with God, which is the significance of Jesus' promise to *"show myself to him"*. This promise is made in the context of the pledge that Jesus would ask the Father to send the Holy Spirit who would be the 'Counsellor' and guide of each believer and of the community of believers.

In the Fourth Gospel this promise of the Holy Spirit who would teach the disciples all things and remind them of everything Jesus had said to them (John 14.26) led to his teaching about the centrality of love in 15.9-17 which concludes with a repeat of the words *"This is my command: Love each other."*

There is probably no more important passage in the Gospels than this for understanding the mind of Jesus and his revelation of the Father. It begins in verse 9 with the statement *"As the Father has loved me so have I loved you"* and the promise that if we obey the commands of Jesus we remain in his love just as he remains in the love of the Father. He then repeats his command that the disciples must love each other as he loved them. He further illustrates this by foreshadowing his own death: *"Greater love has no one than this, that he lay down his life for his friends."*

John 15.13

This is a statement of enormous significance that can only be understood in the context of the social history of Rome. Jesus lived in a time of revolutionary socio-cultural and economic change. It was the last days of the old Roman Republic and the birth pangs of the Roman Empire. In the Republic the monopoly of political power rested with the aristocratic families. This power was usurped by Augustus around the time of the birth of Jesus but it was not until the time of Nero, some 60 years later, that the transformation to Empire was complete.

Household System

Throughout this transitional period the great aristocratic families that had been the building blocks of the Roman Republic provided the model for the Empire in that Augustus transferred the absolute authority exercised by the *pater familias* (head of household) into a dictatorship of the entire Empire. Augustus used the family-centred system to legitimise his political dictatorship while at the same time preserving the basic social characteristics of the Republic. The household system, which was a familiar institution throughout the Greco-Roman world, was a community that recognised the authority of the head of household while also having a clearly defined hierarchy of authority that included a variety of social ranks such as senior stewards, servants, slaves, tenants, as well as relatives, freedmen and friends of the householder.[7]

The 'friends' of the householder occupied an undefined role and could be drawn from any of the social ranks, including slaves, but exercised enormous influence as counsellors and confidantes of the *pater familias*. The friend relied entirely upon the trust and loyalty of his position. If that were called into question he would immediately fall from grace and he and his family would suffer impoverishment, banishment or death. This is the significance of the scarcely veiled blackmail implied at the trial of Jesus before Pilate when the chief priests and their officials shouted, *"If you let this man go, you are no friend of Caesar".*   John 19.12

Jesus would have been perfectly familiar with the household system of the Roman Republic, which was not unlike that of the traditional Hebraic family system that had been practised in Israel since the time of Abraham. His disciples would have understood the uniqueness of the statement he made to emphasise and illustrate the centrality of love among them. *"Greater love has no one than this, that he lay down his life for his friends".*   John 15.13

For the master of the household to sacrifice his life for one of his friends was inconceivable! In acceptable convention it was the friend who should lay down his life for his master. This is yet another convention that Jesus turned upside-down! The friend owed everything to his master while having no status of his own. Apart from the master he was nothing. He and his family were entirely dependent upon the grace and favour of the master whom he served with unquestioning loyalty and obedience.

The Role of the Friend

In the Fourth Gospel this statement is placed in the context of the teaching Jesus gave to his disciples as they sat around the remains of the meal after Judas had left them and gone out

---

[7] Clifford Hill, **'The Sociology of the New Testament Church to AD 62'**, A Doctoral Thesis, University of Nottingham, 1972, pages 207 – 227

into the night to carry out his act of betrayal. Jesus, their master, had washed their feet, a duty usually carried out by the humblest slaves, thus reversing a traditional role of physical service.

Now he reverses the most important intellectual/spiritual role of confidante and counsellor to the master of the household. *"You are my friends"* he said *"if you do what I command"* John 15.14 and his command was simply that they should love one another as he had loved them, which included that he was about to die for them.

Jesus then reminded them of the role of the friend in the household community. He was in a position of enormous responsibility and enjoyed the total confidence and trust of his master to the extent that no secrets were kept from him. All the information about the work of the household, its function in the wider community both social and economic came into the conversation between the master and the friend. Hence Jesus emphasises, *"I no longer call you servants, because the servant does not know his master's business. Instead I have called you friends"*. John 15.15

This is a statement of enormous spiritual significance in which Jesus was stating that the whole revelation of the nature and purposes of God which had been entrusted to him he was now sharing with his disciples.This was nothing less than the incarnation of the Word of God into the household of faith. In order to impress the significance of what he was now entrusting to his disciples he added, *"For everything that I have learned from my Father I have made known to you"*. John 15.15

The full extent of the revelation of God that Jesus possessed he gave to his disciples. He held nothing back and this revelation would soon be completed through the sacrifice of his body and blood. This meant that unlike the prophets, who had each received a part of the revelation of God necessary to their mission in their own particular time and circumstances, the disciples were being commissioned to carry out the Messianic mission to the world.

Jesus warned that if the world hated them they should constantly remember that it hated him first of all and that if they belonged to the world the world would love them.[8]

---

[8] See John 15.18

The Chosen Ones

In order to bring home the distinction between the world and the community of the Kingdom of which they were the pioneers Jesus again, in the next verse, emphasised *"you do not belong to the world, but I have chosen you out of the world"*. This is a repetition for the sake of emphasis of verse 16 *"you did not choose me, but I chose you"*. The significance of this statement is that the usual custom for any potential student wishing to study the Torah was that he would choose the strand of teaching that most appealed to him. The student would listen to the teaching of the rabbis and compare their interpretation of the tradition of the sages. They would then choose the rabbi under whom they wished to study.

Jesus had taken advantage of this practice when he had gone up to Jerusalem with his parents and the community of pilgrims from Galilee at the time of his pre-bar mitzvah visit. He had become so engrossed listening to the teaching of the rabbis in the courts of the temple that he had not noticed that his parents had already left the City. No doubt Paul, in the days of his youth may have had a similar experience as an eager student keen to learn as much as possible of the faith of his forefathers, and had sat at the feet of a number of rabbis before choosing Professor Gamaliel as his mentor.

Jesus reversed this practice in line with innumerable other things that he turned upside down. He did not sit in the temple teaching day by day waiting for men to come and choose to be his disciples. He went out and found a bunch of ordinary men among the working classes, some of whom had already responded to the message of his cousin John who was baptising near the place where the Jordan ran into the Dead Sea, east of the River. We do not know the basis on which Jesus chose his disciples or the criteria for which he was looking. But the one thing we do know is that they did not choose Jesus - **he chose them!** This was obviously of great significance to Jesus as he twice stated the fact that he had chosen them, adding that he had appointed them to *"go and bear fruit"* - fruit that would last.[9]

---

[9] See John 15.16

Lasting Fruit

This reference to *"fruit that will last"* is also of great significance in Jesus' preparation of his disciples for their mission. Unlike the Synoptics there is no 'Great Commission' in the Fourth Gospel but this statement that they were appointed to go and bear fruit that would last is the equivalent. It is a call to evangelism. Just as the fruit of an apple tree is not an apple; and the fruit of a pear tree is not a pear; they are seeds. The fruit of an apple tree is another apple tree! In the same way the fruit of discipleship is not preaching the word, or doing good deeds, or even exercising the spiritual gifts. That is simply handling the seed of the gospel.

The fruit of discipleship is another disciple. It is actually bringing someone into the Kingdom. That is the fruit that will last. If we do not produce fruit that will last we are not a true disciple. When we are proficient in producing lasting fruit Jesus promises that whatever we ask in his name the Father will fulfil. He then repeated, *"This is my command: Love each other."* [10]

The command to love obviously made a huge impact upon the writers of the New Testament as the word 'love' occurs hundreds of times in the Gospels and letters, including 44 times in the first letter of John. Paul's 'ode to love' in 1 Corinthians 13 is one of the most beautiful pieces of literature ever written, full of grace and truth. It captures the heart of the gospel -

"Love is patient, love is kind. It does not envy, it does not boast, it is not proud. It is not rude, it is not self-seeking, it is not easily angered, it keeps no record of wrongs. Love does not delight in evil but rejoices with the truth. It always protects, always trusts, always hopes, always perseveres. Love never fails."

1 Corinthians 13.4 - 8

The Centrality of Love

It was because Paul had so clearly understood Jesus' teaching about love that he was able to explain the significance of the death of Jesus in the context of God's saving love. In Romans 5.5 f he says that *"God has poured out his love into our hearts by the Holy Spirit whom he has given us. You see, at just the right time when we were still powerless, Christ died for the ungodly"*.

---

[10] See John 15.17

He speaks about God demonstrating his own love through the death of Jesus for sinful humanity. In his great prayer of intercession in Ephesians 3.14 f, Paul expresses the centrality of love for the Christian community. He prays that the believers in Ephesus *"being rooted and established in love, may have power, together with all the saints to grasp how wide and long and high and deep is the love of Christ, and to know this love that surpasses knowledge"* so that they may be filled to overflowing with the fullness of God.

In the First Letter of John 'love' is the dominant feature of the whole letter. The Apostle urges his readers not to love the world or anything in the world because he sees that as a barrier to the presence of God in the life of a believer. *"If anyone loves the world, the love of the Father is not in him"* 1 John 2.15. He says this, not simply because *"the cravings of sinful men"* are a distraction from the life of discipleship; but because the very essence of the nature of God is love and all the values and the lusts and ambitions of sinful men are at war with the Spirit of God.

In a passage that reminds us so clearly of the teaching of the great prophets of Israel and that of Jesus, the Apostle says, *"How great is the love the Father has lavished on us that we should be called children of God! And that is what we are!"* 1 John 3.1. He then reminds his readers that there are different spirits that can influence or even possess us. He urges that every spirit should be tested to see if it is from God [11]. The test is whether or not the spirit acknowledges the Lordship of Jesus. But he emphasises the centrality of love saying that love comes from God and *"whoever does not love does not know God because God is love."*   1 John 4.8

This statement that 'God is Love' expresses the heart of the message of the prophets of Israel that was completed and made perfect in the person and work of Messiah Jesus, Son of God our Saviour. It brings us inevitably to the questions raised in Chapter 10 concerning the crucifixion of Jesus and our understanding of the message of Isaiah 53 in light of the witness of Jesus and the writers of the New Testament.

This will be examined in the next chapter.

---

[11] See 1 John 4.1

Unbreakable *Love*

GOD'S TRANSFORMING LOVE AND JUSTICE

This chapter examines how the love of God has acted to break the power of human sin and to bring us into a right relationship with himself. It unpacks the Hebraic background to Paul's teaching on the law, grace and the atonement with special mention of the rabbinic teaching on the 'Second Adam' and the Messianic mission to transform the whole natural order of creation.

Hebraic Roots

We noted in Chapter Ten that there is a sharp difference between the Western understanding of justice and the Hebraic, which lies at the root of the different interpretations of the cross and the concept of the atonement.

In the English language there are two word groups that derive from the same Hebraic root. One group, which comes from the Latin, includes the words 'just', 'justify' and 'justification' which are usually used in a socio-political context. The second group, which comes from the Anglo-Saxon, includes the words 'right', 'righteous' and 'righteousness' and are usually used in a moral, ethical or a religious context. In the Bible all these words come from the same root – *tsadaq* - which has the basic meaning of 'justice'. In the New Testament *tsadaq* is rendered in the Greek as *dikaiosune*.

Unfortunately *dikaiosune* was translated in the Authorised Version as 'righteousness' rather than 'justice' which is followed by most English translations including the NIV. In fact, the word 'justice' does not appear anywhere in the New Testament in the AV and this has distorted our understanding of Paul's teaching on a number of crucial subjects. The Eighteenth Century Cruden's Concordance of the Authorised Version defines the meaning of the word 'justice' as "That essential perfection in God, whereby he is infinitely righteous and just, both in his nature and in all his proceedings with his creatures." It further defines 'justice' as "That political virtue that renders to every man his due and is 'distributive justice'." [1] This definition perfectly illustrates the extent to which the Eighteenth Century Western Church had departed from the Hebraic root of biblical interpretation even in its basic understanding of the nature of God [2].

Justice and Right Relationships

In the Old Testament 'justice' is central to the revelation of the nature of God. If we do not get our understanding of justice in line with what the Bible says we cannot understand the nature of God or his purposes as he determined to work them out through Israel as the Servant of the Lord. As we noted in Chapter Nine, *tsadaq* – justice - is to do with relationships. [3] The just man is one who is in a right relationship with God and with his fellow human beings. This is why Jesus emphasised that the most important command in the Torah was to love God and one's neighbour. All relationships have obligations and responsibilities the fulfilling of which in biblical terms constitutes 'justice'.This is of tremendous importance for understanding the revelation of God in the Old Testament which forms the foundation for the New Testament.

In the teaching of the prophets God revealed himself through what he **DID** as much as through what he said. For the prophets the deeds of the Lord were the easiest way of teaching the people to understand the nature of God. It was through his deeds that God was known to be a Saviour. His greatest act of salvation was in bringing his people out of Egypt.

The prophets never tired of reminding people that this showed that God cared for the poor and powerless, that he hated oppression and injustice, and that he responded to the cries for help from his people with whom he had made a covenant. His justice was seen in the fulfilling of his covenant promises. He overthrew the power of the oppressor to set his people free so that they, on their part, could fulfil their covenant responsibilities enshrined in their relationship with him.

---

[1] **Cruden's Concordance of the Authorised Version of the Bible,** Third Edition, Frederick Warne & Co, London, 1769

[2] The first edition of **Cruden's Concordance** was published in London in 1737

[3] See Chapter 9, page 133 - 136

Justice and the Covenant

The justice of God was seen in some surprising ways which show the inadequacy of using the word 'righteousness', with its moral connotation, instead of 'justice'. But first, we have to understand the nature of the covenant between God and Israel. It was not bilateral; it was unilateral. The terms of the covenant were not the result of negotiation. It was a covenant made by God who chose Israel as the instrument through whom he would reveal himself, his nature and purposes, to all the nations. God promised that he would show unbreakable love to his people. In return they were to be faithful to him, having no other gods and would follow his teaching – the Torah.

The remarkable thing about the justice of God is that although Israel, his people, were unfaithful time after time and failed to observe his teaching, he never ceased to love and to respond to them in accordance with his covenant obligations. Throughout the Old Testament this is not seen as an **act of mercy** but a demonstration of the **justice** of God! It was something he had promised to do and he was faithful in keeping the terms of his covenant relationship even when his people had broken their obligations.

God not only forgave transgressions but he kept no record of the wrongdoings of his people. Hence God could say, *"I, even I, am he who blots out your transgressions, for my own sake, and remembers your sins no more".*   Isaiah 43.25

The phrase "for my own sake" means that God had to act in this way to preserve his own integrity. Micah asked *"Who is a God like you who pardons sin and forgives the transgression of the remnant of his inheritance? You do not stay angry for ever... you will tread our sins underfoot and hurl all our iniquities into the sea"* Micah 7.18-19 And the Psalmist rejoices, *"If you, O Lord, kept a record of sin, O Lord, who could stand? But with you there is forgiveness".*
                                                        Psalm 130.3 - 4

Jeremiah saw this complete forgiveness as one of the central features of the new covenant in which God said *"For I will forgive their wickedness and will remember their sins no more".*
                                                        Jeremiah 31.34

Justice and Forgiveness

Jeremiah's emphasis upon complete forgiveness is reflected in Paul's teaching on the love of God in 1 Corinthians 13 where he says that *'love keeps no record of wrongs'*. Forgiveness is only complete when there is no record kept of the wrongdoing. How often in our own relationships with others do we only grudgingly forgive, and then remind the transgressor at a later date? But God does not keep harping back to previous transgressions although we sin time after time: his free forgiveness blots out the record and leaves us with a clean sheet. That is unbreakable love! But the most remarkable thing is that in God's vocabulary that is *'justice'!*

We misunderstand the nature of God's justice when we interpret the Hebraic Scriptures in accordance with our Western vocabulary. This is of particular significance for understanding the atonement through which God brings salvation to his people and demonstrates his **justice**. For example, the Psalmist prays, *"Deliver me in your justice"* Psalm 31.1 but this is given quite a different meaning in the NIV and other English translations where it is rendered *"Deliver me in your righteousness"*, which implies that there is a moral obligation upon God to act in this way.

There are several similar passages in Isaiah where God says, *"I am bringing my justice near, it is not far away; and my salvation will not be delayed"* Isaiah 46.13 *"My justice draws near speedily, my salvation is on the way and my arm will bring justice to the nations"* Isaiah 51.5 which means that God is about to fulfil his covenant responsibilities. And in 61.10 the prophet rejoices *"For he has clothed me with garments of salvation and arrayed me with a robe of justice"*.

In each of these key passages English translations, such as the NIV, use the word 'righteousness' which has moral or ethical connotations and misses the point which Isaiah is making that this is a demonstration of God's justice. It is **justice** that brings the sinner into a right relationship with God, not because the sinner has earned his reprieve, but because God is exercising his unbreakable love. In so doing God is not showing 'mercy' but 'justice' in that he is acting in accordance with his covenant promises and fulfilling his desire to have his covenant people in a close and intimate relationship with himself which has been broken by human sin. When God acts to bring his people back into a right relationship, that action is 'justification' - they have been 'justified' – they are 'just' - standing in a right relationship with God.

Justice and the Law in Paul's Teaching

When we get a clear understanding of God's justice in its Hebraic setting we can turn to the New Testament with a clearer mindset. In particular we are better able to understand the teaching of Paul whose thinking is grossly misunderstood when forced into a modern Western culture. Although he was a Roman citizen and understood the Roman social system the whole context of Paul's theological thinking is Hebraic which came from his training as a Pharisee under Rabbi Gamaliel.

First, however, it is essential to understand Paul's use of the term 'law' because the justice of God revealed to us in the gospel is not a justice based on law but upon grace.

In Romans 3.21 Paul makes this clear. He says *"But now a justice (dikaiosune) from God, apart from law, has been made known to which the law and the prophets testify. This justice (dikaiosune) from God comes through faith in Jesus Christ to all who believe."*

The NIV and other English translations render this *"now a 'righteousness' from God"* yet in the next verse the same word (dikaiosune) is translated 'justice' - *"He did this to demonstrate his justice"* which tends to convey confusion rather than clarity.

At the risk of boring readers with repetition it is necessary to stress the importance of recognising that in our Western culture the word 'righteousness' usually carries an ethical meaning which is not what Paul is saying here. He is not speaking about right and wrong as defined in our Western legal system. He is contrasting law and grace. He is saying that God's justice - his act of bringing us into a right relationship with himself - does not come through the law - the Torah. He says that both the Prophets and the Torah itself testify to this; that God's act of 'justifying' sinful humanity comes through faith in Jesus the Messiah, not through keeping the law – the regulations of the Torah. It is important to remember that Paul is not speaking of the Latin civil law as we understand it in the West. He is referring to God's law - to obeying 'God's teaching', the Torah.

In order to understand Paul's teaching in Romans we have to see it in the context of his purpose in writing the letter to a community where there was a bitter dispute between Gentile and Jewish Christians. This largely concerned whether or not Gentile believers should be required to conform to the law in regard to such things as circumcision and dietary regulations. Rows had broken out in the synagogues, which had spilled over into the streets, coming to the attention of the authorities.

The Jews were blamed for the disturbances that led to the Emperor Claudius issuing an edict expelling Jews from the City of Rome in AD 45. This lasted about five years before they began drifting back, but in that time the Gentile congregation of the church in Rome had grown considerably, but relationships with Jewish believers in Jesus had not improved. The Messianic Jews believed they were superior to the Gentile believers because they were the chosen people of the covenant.

Paul's purpose in writing Romans is to counter this. He asks, *"Where, then, is boasting? It is excluded. On what principle? On that of observing the law? No, but on that of faith"* Romans 3.27. He insists that God justifies both the circumcised and the uncircumcised through the same faith in Messiah Jesus.

Law and Grace

Paul further emphasises the faith basis of salvation by saying that *"It was not through law that Abraham and his offspring received the promise that he would be heir of the world, but through the justification that comes by faith".*   Romans 4.13

He sees Abraham not only as the father of Jews but as the father of all who come into a right relationship with God through faith. His purpose in saying this is not to undermine the uniqueness of faith in Jesus, but to stress the distinction between law and grace. Paul sees the law as powerless to save us from death – which is separation from God. In Galatians 3.6-3.29 he elaborates this, saying that **all** who believe are children of Abraham. *"The Scripture foresaw that God would justify the Gentiles by faith, and announced the gospel in advance to Abraham: 'All nations will be blessed through you'."* He adds, *"If you belong to Christ, then you are Abraham's seed, and heirs according to the promise"* Galatians 3.29. Paul says that the law was to point us to Jesus: *"It was put in charge to lead us to Christ that we might be justified by faith".*   Galatians 3.24

Once Jesus came, the law had achieved its purpose. That does not mean that the law was redundant or abrogated but simply that it had fulfilled its purpose in the same way as a guardian cared for a minor until he came of age and could inherit what had been promised by his father. Dwight Pryor gives an Hebraic interpretation of Jesus' words in the Sermon on the Mount, *"Do not think I have come to abolish the law or the Prophets; I have not come to abolish them but to fulfil them".*   Matthew 5.17

Pryor says that Jesus was not saying that the Torah was now redundant, that it had fulfilled its purpose, and therefore could be discarded. He says "'Abolish' and 'fulfil' were technical rabbinic terms at the time, meaning: 'I have not come to misinterpret the Torah, so as to undermine it or abolish it. I have come to properly interpret the Torah, so as to lead to right conduct and thereby bring the Torah to its intended fulfilment'." [5]

Paul, of course, would have understood Jesus' words in their Hebraic context, so he would not have been advocating discarding the Torah. He nevertheless warned that you cannot simply obey a part of the law, as the Galatians wished to do, by becoming circumcised and continuing to live as Gentiles in all other respects. He quoted Deuteronomy 27.26 *"Cursed is everyone who does not continue to do everything written in the Book of the Law".*

Galatians 3.10

Jesus and the Law

Paul knew that in the eyes of the Priests and Pharisees, the upholders of the law, Jesus was a lawbreaker.[6] As they saw things, he did not observe the Sabbath, he broke the dietary rules by eating with people whom the law classed as sinners, he revised basic requirements of the law, *"you have heard it said... but I say to you"*; worst of all, he claimed to forgive sins thus making himself equal with God. It was this that terrified Pilate when the Chief Priests and their officials said *"We have a law and according to that law he must die, because he claimed to be the Son of God".*

John 19.7

---

[5] Dwight A Pryor, **A Different God?**, CFI Communications, Eastbourne, 2007

[6] Jesus kept to the purest teachings of the Torah, but not to the 'extra laws' introduced over time by the religious leaders to 'ring fence' the Torah God had initially given. It was these extra 'man made' laws that Jesus didn't adhere to, in order to discredit them compared with the true Torah of God.

Paul said that Jesus was *"born under the law, to redeem those under the law"* Galatians 4.4. He was crucified with lawbreakers on either side of him: *"he was counted with the lawless ones"* [7] Mark 15.28. He was put to death under the law by the upholders of the law. His was no sham assumption of transgressing the law. He suffered capital punishment for breaking the law.

No doubt when Paul held the coats of the young men who set about stoning Stephen to death he thought that it was right to deal with lawbreakers in this way. He knew the scripture *"Cursed is everyone who is hung on a tree"* because he quoted it in Galatians 3.13. At that time all Jerusalem was buzzing with accounts of the resurrection of Jesus but Paul discounted them. He didn't believe it until Jesus met with him on the road to Damascus.

That changed everything. The shocking reality blinded Paul. Jesus was alive! His worst fears became a reality – Jesus was the Messiah and through raising him from the dead God had vindicated his Messiah. The arrogant law enforcer was stunned; left blindly staggering into the city seeking shelter where he had come to murder the believers in *Jesus*. Nothing would ever be the same again.

Paul and the Law

Through his Damascus Road experience Paul himself was identified with Christ's death. He too had died to the law through the Cross. His testimony was *"I died to the law so that I might live for God. I have been crucified with Christ and I no longer live, but Christ lives in me"*.   Galatians 2.19 - 20

He needed to go away alone to rethink his whole theology. He saw that it was zeal for the law that had actually led to the murderous crime of Calvary committed by the religious leaders of Israel with whom he was identified. The very law by which he lived and breathed had become to him 'a body of death' Romans 7.24. He realised that he would not have known what sin was except through the law, so that the law actually became the means of robbing him of life and making him 'a slave to sin'.

This later became an important part of his testimony to the believers in Rome. He said, " *I see another law at work in the members of my body, waging war against the law of my mind*

---

[7] NIV margin and Isaiah 53.12

and making me a prisoner of the law of sin at work within my members" Romans 7.23. But he was overwhelmed with thanksgiving to God for what Jesus the Messiah had done. *"Through Christ Jesus the law of the Spirit of life set me free from the law of sin and death".*
                                                                    Romans 8.2

Paul then continues by saying that what the law was powerless to do God achieved by sending his own Son. The NIV says that Jesus came *"in the likeness of sinful man to be a sin offering"* Romans 8.3. But the Greek makes no mention of *"a sin offering"*. This is an insertion of the translators to give credibility to their (penal substitution) theological interpretation of the Cross. The AV does not say this. It is literally closer to the Greek: *"For what the law could not do, in that it was weak through the flesh, God sending his own son in the likeness of sinful flesh, and for sin, condemned sin in the flesh."*

Paul says that this was *"in order that the act of justice of the law might be fulfilled in us, who do not walk according to the flesh but according to the Spirit "*[8]. The NIV's use of the term "the righteous requirements of the law" is misleading. Again, the AV is closer to the Greek but it too uses the word "righteousness" instead of "act of justice" which shows the influence of Western culture and a lack of understanding of the Hebraic content of the New Testament.

Paul and the Cross

If we take these important statements in the context of Paul's Hebraic theology and his other references to the law and the death of Christ we find that Paul is proclaiming freedom from the law because the law was unable to achieve the very purpose for which it was given - to act as 'guardian' until the coming of Messiah - so the law itself had become associated with sin. Paul says *"the sting of death is sin, and the power of sin is the law".*
                                                            1 Corinthians 15.56

A similar thought is expressed in Hebrews 2.14f which refers to the death of Christ saying *"that by his death he might destroy him who holds the power of death - that is, the devil - and free those who all their lives were held in slavery by their fear of death."* The death of Christ upon the Cross did much more than just liberate those who were under the power of the law. It actually

---

[8] Author's translation

achieved something for the whole human race and not simply for the covenant people of God who were descendants of Abraham after the flesh, as was Paul. Through the death and resurrection of Jesus something actually happened to break the power of sin that was separating the whole of humanity from God and leading to death.

Something momentous happened in the spiritual realm. Paul says that *"Sin entered the world through one man, and death through sin, and in this way death came to all men"*.   Romans 5.12

He says that as death came to all humanity through one man, life has now become available to all people through the person of Jesus. He says that *" For if, by the trespass of the one man, death reigned through that one man, how much more will those who receive God's abundant provision of grace and of the gift of justification (NIV 'righteousness') reign in life through the one man, Jesus Christ"*.   Romans 5.17

The death and resurrection of Jesus makes it possible for all human beings to enter into a right relationship with God through faith in Jesus. The teaching of the New Testament is that the whole of humanity is subject to death; that all are sinners, which implies that all are separated from God and therefore from life. No doubt this is why Jesus himself says that no one comes to the Father except through him. [9] Through the Cross Jesus broke the curse of death that hangs over the whole of humanity and has made it possible for people of all nations to enter into a new and living relationship with God that lasts through all eternity.

Paul spells this out clearly in Ephesians where he says that together with the whole of humanity *"we were by nature objects of wrath"* Ephesians 2.3 Then in the next verse he adds, *"But because of his great love for us, God, who is rich in mercy, made us alive with Christ even when we were dead in transgressions."* The Cross undoubtedly is a demonstration of how far God will go to show his love to those whom he created in his own image; but it is also much more than that. It is the way to life; indeed, if we accept the testimony of Jesus, it is the ***only*** way.

We must conclude therefore that the vast majority of humanity remains separated from God at the conclusion of their earthly life. This is the teaching of the prophets, of the Gospels and the writers

---

[9] See John 14.6

of the New Testament. If we believe their teaching it should surely give us the drive to communicate the Word of life to our friends and neighbours and all whom we love.

What happens to those who die in separation from God? Are they snuffed out of existence? Or, which is surely far worse, do they go to a place where they live in a torment of regret for the past, as in Jesus' parable of the rich man and Lazarus[10]. Speculation upon such questions would be outside the scope of this book. But for those who care deeply for someone who has no faith, who has not been *"raised up with Christ"*,[11] these are disturbing questions that ought to be faced.

The Reformation and Law

The great Reformers, Luther and Calvin, who did so much to liberate believers from the spiritual bankruptcy of the Church in their day, and the intellectual absolutism of the Pope, rightly emphasised the basis of salvation by faith and faith alone. They were, nevertheless, still subject to the Latin culture of law which had dominated the Western world since the days of the Roman Empire. Luther saw three uses of the law.

The first - was to bring us to the point of despair as he himself had done when realising that there was no way that he could be justified before God by keeping the rules of the Church or of his own monastic order.

The second - was to lead us to Christ as Paul describes in Galatians.

The third - was to give Christians a rule for life after they have been justified by faith in Christ.

Thus orthodox Protestant teaching was characterised by two features - its doctrine of justification by faith; and its doctrine of the law. The law became that which was given to Moses at Sinai but without the Jewish feasts and festivals, and ceremonial prescriptions. The Puritans took the Ten Commandments and used them as the basis of law, which they elaborated in some detail as providing the basic rules of life.

---

[10] See Luke 16.19 - 31

[11] See Ephesians 2.6

Protestant theology became dominated by law despite its emphasis upon grace and the claim that salvation is only to be found through faith in Christ. Paul's statement *"It is by grace you have been saved"* Ephesians 2.5 was the bedrock of Reformation theology. Nevertheless, 'righteousness' became defined as conformity to the law. In fact Calvin claimed that the righteousness of Christ lay in his perfect obedience to the law and he endorsed Anselm's Christology that through the Cross Jesus rendered 'satisfaction' to the law that required the death of the sinner. Protestant theology became firmly centred around a penal substitution view of the Cross which has survived until this day.

The Reformation which aimed to de-sanctify Christianity by breaking the mediatory power of the priests and enabling every believer to have a direct personal relationship with Jesus, did not, in fact, take us back to New Testament Christianity because it failed to understand and embrace the Hebraic revelation of God which runs not only through the Old Testament but through the Gospels and all the writers of the New Testament as well.

Western Christianity became a law-based religion and this largely influenced the theology of the Cross. God's greatest act of salvation in fulfilment of his covenant promise to show unconditional love to the human beings he had created in his own image, was changed from an act of love creating 'at-one-ment' to the fulfilment of a legal requirement. Reformation teaching was that the law demanded that the sinner should be punished by death and Jesus took the place of all sinners in order to satisfy the law. But is this really what Paul meant?

The Atonement

Anselm, Archbishop of Canterbury from 1093 to 1109, was the first theologian to develop what became known as the penal substitution theory of the cross which was a rational explanation of the death of Christ. He did not appeal to Scripture. His entire systemic reasoning was based on Latin civil law, derived from Roman law, rather than biblical evidence.

Anslem reasoned that God was offended by human sin and in order for forgiveness to be offered it was necessary for Christ to die so that the demands of God's 'justice' would be satisfied. The sacrifice of Jesus, through the shedding of his blood upon cross, was necessary in order to satisfy the wrath of God. This is the interpretation of the atonement that is embraced by most evangelicals today.

This theory was challenged in Anselm's own day by **Peter Abelard** (1079-1142) whose view of the atonement became known as the 'moral influence theory'. He said that God identified with sinful humanity by dying on the cross and showing how much he loves us so that we would be moved to repentance and live a life of obedience.

Many theologians have followed this view including such outstanding scholars as **C H Dodd**. In his commentary on Romans 5.12-21 Dodd says that Jesus "lived a wonderful life, and died a death of perfect self-sacrifice... he has thereby given an inspiring example... through the moral achievement of Christ all men may rise to goodness." Today such a view is largely identified with liberal theologians. But surely if Jesus came simply as an example for us, he came for our damnation rather than our salvation, for we can never achieve his sinless perfection!

Dodd further states in reference to an Abelardian view of the cross, "It is a good enough argument for those who accept the rabbinic doctrine of the Fall."[12] He says that Paul was influenced by the rabbinic concept of corporate responsibility for sin, as when Achan's sin resulted in the punishment of his whole family.[13]

This is how he interprets Paul's statement *"For if the many died by the trespass of the one man, how much more did God's grace and the gift that came by the grace of the one man, Jesus Christ, overflow to the many!"*   Romans 5.15

Messianic Age

Dodd is right in describing the new dispensation of the Messianic Age inaugurated by Christ as familiar in first century Judaism but this was largely confined to thinking among the rabbis because non-rabbis were discouraged from studying texts such as Genesis 1.2 and Ezekiel 1.4 ff which, according to **W D Davies** were regarded by the rabbis as "cosmological speculation" and as "a menace to religious faith".[14]

---

[12] C H Dodd, **Moffat New Testament Commentary**, The Epistle of Paul to the Romans, Hodder and Stoughton, London, 1947, page 79

[13] See Joshua 7

The reason why the rabbis discouraged what they called 'cosmological speculation' was due to the rise of interest in the Messianic Age and the doctrine of the Fall of Adam depicted in Genesis. This interest arose in the post-exilic period and continued right up to the time of Jesus. **Oesterley and Robinson** say that the exile itself "contributed to a deep sense of sin" in the nation.[15] Nehemiah recounts that when the Book of the Law was read to the people there was a great deal of weeping [16], and even more expressive is the lamentation in Isaiah 64.6 *"All of us have become like one who is unclean, and all our righteous acts are like filthy rags".*

It was out of this sense of national shame that, after the return from Babylon, interest arose in the origins of sin and in the redemptive work of Messiah. There was a corporate longing for a national cleansing which would be accomplished by Messiah. But interest in the transformational work of Messiah goes right back to Isaiah of Jerusalem in the eighth century where the coming of Messiah is prophesied to inaugurate a new era in which *" the wolf will live with the lamb and the leopard will lie down with the goat,"* Isaiah 11.2 – an era that would transform the whole natural order of creation.

Cosmic Transformation

Some 200 years after Isaiah of Jerusalem, in the period leading up to the end of the exile in Babylon, the expectation that the Messianic Age would bring about cosmic transformation was growing. This is reflected in Isaiah 55.12f where the prophet announces *" You will go out in joy and be led forth in peace; the mountains and hills will burst into song before you and all the trees of the field will clap their hands."*[17]

This is followed by the significant statement that the natural environment will be transformed, *" Instead of the thorn bush will grow the pine tree, and instead of briars the myrtle will grow"* which reflects the belief that when Adam sinned it was not simply

---

[14] W D Davies, **Paul and Rabbinic Judaism**, SPCK, London, 1955, page 37

[15] Oesterley and Robinson. **Hebrew Religion**, SPCK, London, 1930, page 296

[16] See Nehemiah 8.9

[17] Another passage with a similar picture of cosmic transformation is found in Isaiah 35 where the desert and the wilderness will blossom and the whole of nature will reflect the glory of the Lord.

human beings who were affected but the whole of nature. Animals became carnivorous and instead of fruit trees, thorn bushes and thistles covered the land. Producing food became hard labour for human beings whereas it had been amply provided in the perfect environment of Eden.

All this degrading of nature would be reversed through the advent of Messiah and the new age which he would inaugurate. This is foreseen apocalyptically in post-exilic literature such as Isaiah 65.17f, " *Behold, I will create new heavens and a new earth. The former things will not be remembered, nor will they come to mind.*" What was envisaged was 'a new creation' which is the term Paul used. But it was not only Paul who spoke of a new creation to be inaugurated by Messiah.

The rabbis in Paul's day also taught that the Messianic Age would correspond to a new beginning of all things, the counterpart of Genesis 1.2. The new concept introduced by Paul was to declare that Jesus was a 'Second Adam'. "It was generally recognised that the Messianic Age would correspond to the beginning of all things. This is explicitly set forth in 4 Ezra 7.29, 32: *'And the world shall return to its first silence seven days, as it was at the beginning so that no man is left '.*" [18]

Acts 6.7 tells us that *"a large number of priests became obedient to the faith"* in Jerusalem in the days following Pentecost. They would have been familiar with rabbinic teaching on the Messianic Age but there is no evidence that the term, 'Second Adam' was applied to the Messiah before Paul's teaching. The significance of Paul's words in Romans 5 and 1 Corinthians 15 is that he builds upon the rabbinic teaching of a 'new creation' and speaks of Adam as *"a pattern of the one to come"* Romans 5.14. He then argues, *"just as the result of one trespass was condemnation for all men, so also the result of one act of righteousness was justification that brings life for all men"* Romans 5.18. This is made even more explicit in 1 Corinthians 15.22, *"For as in Adam all die, so in Christ all will be made alive."*

Clearly such a statement cannot be limited to the forgiveness of individual sins when each human being accepts Jesus as Messiah and Lord. Of course, there is an individual element in this, as each one has to take the step of faith in order to enter into the company of believers in Christ and become part of the new creation.

---

[18] W D Davies, ibid, page 39 quoting from the Apocrypha

Paul's teaching on this subject is somewhat obscured and individualised by the NIV translation of 2 Corinthians 5.17. *"Therefore, if anyone is in Christ, he is a new creation; the old has gone, the new has come!"* But a literal translation of the Greek is, *"So that if anyone* [is] *in Christ* [there is] *a new creation; the old things passed away; behold, all things have become new."*

Paul's teaching here is fully in line with rabbinic concepts of the new creation inaugurated by Messiah which is lost in our Western individualism. Paul continues in the same sentence, saying *"and all things are of God, who reconciled us to himself by Jesus Christ and gave to us the ministry* (service) *of reconciliation; how that God was in Christ reconciling the world to himself,"* which surely means the whole order of creation rather than the mere forgiveness of individual sins.

The Messianic Mission
Reconciling the Whole Order of Creation

It is because we have lost so much of the Hebraic background to the New Testament and subjected Paul's teaching to Greek and Latin concepts that we have lost the cosmic scope of the messianic mission of reconciling the whole created order to God which was initiated in the first advent of Jesus and will be completed in his second coming. It is the diminished concept of reconciliation, and the individualisation of salvation, that has obscured our understanding of the atonement and resulted in conflicting theories such as those of Anselm and Abelard which are today represented by western evangelicalism and liberalism.

Steve Chalke's publication in 2003 of his book *"The Lost Message of Jesus"* gave rise to a flurry of debate. In this he said that the cross was not a vengeful father punishing his son but a symbol of love; a demonstration of how far God is prepared to go to prove his love for human beings. "On the cross Jesus took on the ideology that violence is the ultimate solution by turning the other cheek and refusing to return evil for evil, willingly absorbing its impact within his own body". [19]

But while Chalke is right in challenging the concept of a 'vengeful Father punishing his son', his answer is simply a repetition of the liberal view that the cross is a demonstration of God's love.

---

[19] Steve Chalke, **The Lost Message of Jesus**, Oasis, London, 2003, page 179

This is certainly not New Testament teaching and does not reflect the very explicit statements of Paul.

The Cross does indeed show God's unbreakable love but it also **achieves** both the forgiveness of sin for all those who accept Jesus as Lord and Saviour *AND* of infinitely greater significance, upon the cross, when the temple curtain was torn asunder, the veil of death between God and humanity was destroyed. This was the first part of God's act of 'new creation', enabling those whom he has made in his own image, to enter into a state of reconciliation with himself – a new life that begins in the here and now and extends into all eternity.

This act of new creation of human beings was the first action in the Messianic Age which will be fulfilled at the second coming of our Lord when the whole created order will also be reconciled to God and the new order of creation will be transformed from that of apocalyptic vision to present reality.

Then will be fulfilled the hope of the prophets of Israel – 'Immanuel', God with us. So too will be the vision of John on the island of Patmos,

"Then I saw a new heaven and a new earth, for the first heaven and the first earth had passed away... Now the dwelling of God is with men and he will live with them. They will be his people, and God himself will be with them and be their God... He who was seated on the throne said, 'I am making everything new!'"

Revelation 21.1 - 5

Unbreakable *Love*

Chapter Twelve

RE-DISCOVERING THE LOVE OF GOD

This chapter offers a brief summary of the message of the prophets which revealed the nature of God as 'Unbreakable Love'. It shows how the Hebraic background to the New Testament was lost soon after the Apostolic Age and at the Council of Nicaea no one could speak Hebrew and the church lost its roots, with the result that the revelation of the nature of God and his unbreakable love brought through the prophets was lost. It was not recovered in the Reformation and the chapter ends with a plea for a new biblically based Reformation.

The Prophets and the Nature of God

There is no easy way to summarise the teaching of the prophets on the nature of God. Each of the writing prophets has his own distinctive style and the message of each has to be studied in the context of the circumstances of their day. It is notable that each of the writing prophets was called to ministry at a time of national crisis when there was an urgent need for divine guidance. They each contributed to our knowledge of the nature of God and it is possible to discern a progression in the revelation given to these servants of God over a period of some 400 years.

Amos

Amos is the earliest of the eighth century prophets and he began his ministry at a time when the Assyrian Empire was threatening to sweep all the smaller nations of the Middle East into its orbit. His message to the northern kingdom of Israel was essentially one of warning. *"Surely the eyes of the sovereign Lord are on the sinful kingdom"* Amos 9.8. Nevertheless, although most of the message of Amos is dealing sternly with personal immorality among all classes of society, and faithlessness and apostasy, the prophet perceives the sovereignty of God over all nations and his special covenant relationship with the house of Israel. There is no mention of the love of God in the message but there are hints of

God's compassion where Amos twice cries out to the Lord to forgive the nation from the rigours of judgement and God relents.[1]

Hosea

In the same period Hosea also prophesied to Ephraim bringing similar warnings that the nation would suffer under the Assyrians, but there was a tenderness in Hosea's message that was missing in that of Amos. He did not speak directly of the love of God for the nation but there was a beautiful compassion with which he spoke of God's action of caring for Ephraim early in their history although they did not realise it. He reported God saying *"I led them with cords of human kindness, with ties of love"*.   Hosea 11.4

Isaiah of Jerusalem

Similarly, within a few years of Amos and Hosea's ministries, Isaiah of Jerusalem was called to bring the same dire warnings to the southern kingdom of Judah which was also being invaded by the Assyrians. He described the situation as, *"Your country is desolate, your cities burned with fire; your fields are being stripped by foreigners right before you"* Isaiah 1.7. As the threat to Jerusalem grew his message increased in urgency, *"In repentance and rest is your salvation, in quietness and trust is your strength"*.

Isaiah 30.15

He pleaded with the people to trust God saying, *"The Lord longs to be gracious to you; he rises to show you compassion. For the Lord is a God of justice"* Isaiah 30.18. The nearest Isaiah of Jerusalem gets to speaking about the love of God is found in the 'Song of the Vineyard' which begins *"I will sing for the one I love a song about his vineyard"*.   Isaiah 5.1

Jeremiah

Jeremiah is the first to speak directly of the love of God and this is revealed to him on the eve of the destruction of Jerusalem about which he had been forewarning for the whole of his long ministry. As the tragedy became inevitable, in the midst of his grief, Jeremiah heard God promising that the city would be rebuilt after the destruction which had not yet taken place and the people would be brought back from exile to which they had not yet been

---

[1] see Amos 7.1-6

taken. It was in this context that Jeremiah was the first to hear God speaking in explicit terms about his love for his covenant people, *"I have loved you with an everlasting Love; I have drawn you with loving kindness".*   Jeremiah 31.3

The Fatherhood of God

It is after the exile that the extent and depth of the love of God for his people becomes clear in prophetic revelation. The first time God is directly referred to as Father is in the post-exilic section of Isaiah. In what is known as the 'Prayer of Lamentation' there are three references to the Fatherhood of God. In the first two God is said to be the 'Father and Redeemer' who has watched over the nation throughout its history. In contrast to the patriarchs, who are figures of the past, God is said to be alive and active today.[2] In the 'lamentation' the sins of the nation, that had brought judgement upon the people, are starkly acknowledged and lead into the declaration *"Yet, O Lord, you are our Father".*   Isaiah 64.8

It is this revelation of the Fatherhood of God, originating with the post-exilic prophets, that is developed by Jesus and becomes the central feature of his ministry. This is particularly noticeable in the Fourth Gospel where Jesus constantly refers to God as 'Father' and he teaches his disciples about the Fatherly love of God, telling them that as the Father has loved them so they are to love one another.

The whole of the New Testament is a record of the love of God which is dealt with at length in the letters of Paul and in the writings of the other Apostles. John specifically states that *'God is love'*.[3] He goes so far as to say that anyone who does not love his brother, whom he has seen, cannot love God, whom he had not seen. He is even more direct in saying, *"If anyone says, 'I love God', yet hates his brother, he is a liar".*   1 John 4.19

The New Testament

This emphasis upon love that is central to the New Testament stems directly from the teaching of Jesus. In the Fourth Gospel the final week in Jesus' life is spent in teaching his disciples to understand the meaning of love. This is not only in his teaching but also in his actions. Jesus takes a bowl of water and a towel

---

[2] see Isaiah 63.16

[3] see 1 John 4.16

and washes his disciples' feet which is an act of humility and service that prepares the way for his ultimate self-sacrifice on the Cross[4]. In his teaching, which John sets in the context of the Last Supper, Jesus teaches his disciples about the nature of God which is essentially 'love'. He says, *"As the Father has loved me, so have I loved you. Now remain in my love"* John 15.9. At the conclusion of this section he does not just advise his disciples to love each other; on the contrary, he issues it as a command! *"This is my **command**: love each other."* John 15.17

The Meaning of Love

Clearly, it was of tremendous importance to Jesus that his disciples should understand the meaning of love. It was central to his gospel and it was essential that they should put into practice the teaching and the example that he had given to them. The reason for this is that Jesus, in his person, was completing the revelation of the nature and purposes of God given through the prophets of Israel for his covenant people.

Jesus stressed that what the disciples were receiving was not simply his own personal love for them. Through their discipleship they were being brought into a special relationship with God. He said, *"The Father himself loves you because you have loved me and have believed that I came from God. I came from the Father and entered the world; now I am leaving the world and going back to the Father"* John 16.27-28. In this statement Jesus emphasises his own oneness with the Father which he had already referred to in answer to a question from Philip who had asked him to show him the Father. The answer was, *"anyone who has seen me has seen the Father"* John 14.9. This statement defined the incarnation and the relationship of Jesus to God the Father.

Athanasius and Arius

It was statements like this that led to controversies in the creed-making period of the early church and the bitter dispute between Athanasius and Arius. Was Jesus of 'one substance' with the Father or was he created by God? The church leaders who gathered at Nicaea in the year AD 325 rightly perceived that it was essential for the future of Christianity that this question should be settled. Unfortunately, they wasted a great deal of time and energy in a bitter dispute which could have been avoided if they had had

---

[4] see John 13.3 - 11

the necessary scholarship. Athanasius could have demolished the arguments put forward by Arius if he had known Hebrew. Both of them only had the Septuagint [5] and the accounts that we have available of events at Nicaea indicate that there were no Hebrew scholars in the church at that time.

Lost Hebrew Roots

The Fourth Century Church was now entirely Gentile and had not only lost its Jewish members but even more importantly had lost its Hebrew roots. This was of great significance for the continuity of the revelation given through the prophets and through Jesus and the Apostles. The Hellenisation of the gospel resulted in a significant loss of essential features in the nature of God and his purposes both for Israel and the followers of Jesus.

This can be illustrated through a study of the word 'love' in the Hebrew text of the Old Testament in comparison with the LXX translation. For example, in Isaiah 54.10 there is the beautiful statement, *"'Though the mountains be shaken and the hills be removed, yet my unfailing love for you will not be shaken nor my covenant of peace be removed', says the Lord, who has compassion on you."*

The LXX translation of Isaiah 54.10 does not have the word 'love'. It translates the Hebrew *'heseth'* to the Greek *'elyos'*. Thus changing 'love' to 'mercy'. The statement, *"my mercy for you will not be changed"* LXX entirely misses the point and fails to express what is an essential part of the very nature of God which was revealed to the Prophet at a crucial point in the spiritual development of the covenant people of God.

This was not merely a slip in translation but was due to the fact that in Greek there is no word that adequately translates *'heseth'*. For example, in the whole of Homer's Odyssey the word 'love' does not appear. In classical literature the Greeks only had *'philos'* - 'friendship' or *'eros'* - 'lust'. In the Koine [6] there was a verbal form *'ayapene'* but it was rarely used as a noun, *'agape'* – love. The New Testament writers virtually invented the word to express the teaching of Jesus and that of the Apostles.

In English we have an even greater paucity of language. We only

---

[5] The Greek translation referred to as 'LXX' in the rest of this chapter

[6] The common Greek, rather than classical Greek

have one word 'love' to mean everything from physical lust to the unbreakable love of God that took Jesus to the Cross.

Hellenisation

The process of Hellenisation of the church can be seen in its early stages in Paul's letter to the Romans. The Roman Church was characterised by strong divisions between Jews and Gentiles. These disputes centred around the practices of the law such as circumcision and dietary rules. Was it obligatory upon Gentiles to observe these practices? It is entirely possible that some of these arguments which took place in the synagogue spilled out into the streets and were brought to the attention of the Roman authorities and became a contributory factor in the issuing of the Edict of Claudius in AD 45 banishing Jews from Rome. It appears that within about five years many Jews were drifting back to the capital of the Empire but their absence for this period had a profound effect upon the Christian church. The Gentile church had grown and the Jews no doubt did not find it easy to integrate upon their return.

Paul's letter addresses this situation, the heart of which is in chapters 9 to 11. But in chapter 3 Paul asked the rhetorical question *"What advantage, then, is there in being a Jew, or what value is there in circumcision?"* His answer was that there was a great advantage, because the Jews had been entrusted with the revelatory utterances of God. But he concedes that not all Jews had faith in God and that both Jew and Gentile alike are all under sin. This enabled him to reach the central point of his gospel that in Christ God had brought salvation 'apart from the law' and that it is only by faith in Jesus that we can come into a right relationship with God.

Despite this teaching that Jew and Gentile are equal before God, in Romans 14, Paul appears to exacerbate the division by referring to the 'weak' and the 'strong'. This was in reference to what was evidently a sharp division between Jewish believers, who still followed dietary rules and observed the Sabbath and other holy days in the Hebrew calendar, and Gentile believers who boasted that they themselves were free from such legalistic requirements. He refers to the one who eats only vegetables as being weak in the faith; that is implying that the Gentiles who eat anything are stronger in their faith. He declares that he is *"fully convinced that no food is unclean in itself"* Romans 14.14 but that it is wrong for a man to eat anything that causes someone else to stumble.

Paul's concern is that the Gentiles and Jews in the Church at Rome should not judge each other or put stumbling blocks in the way of other believers. But his reference to those *"whose faith is weak"* would hardly have been helpful in creating better relationships within the body of believers. By declaring that he can eat anything he was aligning himself with the Gentiles and relegating the Jewish believers (weak in the faith) to some kind of second-class citizenship within the kingdom of God which was no doubt the last thing that Paul wished to do. His handling of this dispute does, however, give us a glimpse into life in the Church in Rome in those early days. Clearly the process of Hellenisation was already quite well advanced.

Consequences of Hellenisation

I. The One New Man

The consequences of the Hellenisation of the early church were to have far-reaching effects that are still with us today. The most immediate loss was something to which Paul himself was passionately committed. This was the creation of the 'one new man' in Christ Jesus. Paul dealt with it at some length in the letter to the Ephesians where he speaks of it as a 'mystery' that had been part of God's eternal plan from the beginning of creation. This mystery was now being made known to the rulers and authorities in the heavenly realms.[7]

It was a central part of God's plan that the Gentiles who *"were separate from Christ, excluded from citizenship in Israel and foreigners to the covenants of the promise, without hope and without God in the world"* Ephesians 2.12 were now being brought into a new relationship with God alongside Jewish believers in Jesus.

This was breaking down the old enmity because Jesus had destroyed the barriers and created *"in himself one new man out of the two, thus making peace"*. Consequently the Gentiles were *"no longer foreigners and aliens but fellow citizens with God's people and members of God's household, built on the foundation of the apostles and prophets with Christ Jesus himself as the chief cornerstone"*. Ephesians 2.11- 20

---

[7] see Ephesians 1.9-10; and 3.8-12

This bringing together of Jew and Gentile in one body of faith, brought about through the shed blood of the Lord Jesus, which Paul saw as central to God's plan of salvation for humanity was rapidly lost as the age-old hostilities continued and became doctrinal battlegrounds. Paul's hope was that the reconciling of Jew and Gentile in Christ would be the first stage in the re-creation, or re-harmonisation of the whole natural order that had been lost through Adam's transgression. He saw the whole creation in bondage to sin and decay and crying out for its liberation which would not happen until Jew and Gentile came together in a spiritual union as sons of God.[8]

II. Hebraic Roots

The second consequence of the Hellenisation of the Early Church was the loss of the Hebraic roots of the gospel which Paul saw as providing continuity with the promises given to Israel through the prophets. Jeremiah had prophesied that the day would come when God would establish a New Covenant that would be written in the hearts of people rather than on tablets of stone, and everyone would know God for themselves. [9]

Clearly this had been made possible through the outpouring of the Holy Spirit at Pentecost, and in Galatians Paul developed the theme that the Gentiles shared in the covenant promises given to Israel when they came to faith through Jesus. He declared *"You are all sons of God through faith in Christ Jesus, for all of you who were baptised into Christ have clothed yourself with Christ."* Galatians 3.26 From this he was able to affirm, *"There is neither Jew nor Greek, slave nor free, male nor female, for you are all one in Christ Jesus. If you belong to Christ, then you are Abraham's seed and heirs according to the promise".*   Galatians 3.29

This last statement is of great significance in Paul's understanding of the purposes of God and how they were to be worked out through the spiritual unity of Jew and Gentile in the body of Christ. This is fully in line with the prophecies in Isaiah that the people of Israel would be a light for the Gentiles.[10] Paul actually quoted this verse when addressing the congregation in the synagogue at Pisidian Antioch.

---

[8] see Romans 8.18-25

[9] see Jeremiah 31.31f

The report in Acts 13.42f says that *"On the next Sabbath almost the whole city gathered to hear the word of the Lord. When the Jews saw the crowds, they were filled with jealousy and talked abusively against what Paul was saying"*. Paul and Barnabas nevertheless spoke boldly saying that they had been right in going first to the synagogue, but as their message was being rejected they would now turn to the Gentiles. Paul said *"For this is what the Lord has commanded us: 'I have made you a light for the Gentiles, that you may bring salvation to the ends of the earth'"*. Acts 13.47

It was clearly Paul's understanding that the Gentiles would share with the Jews in the covenant promises originally given to Israel, but not take them over. He saw this as a fulfilment of what had been revealed to the prophets, that the people of Israel should be the means through which God **extended** his salvation to the whole world. It was a continual grief to Paul that in so many cities on his itinerary where he faithfully went first to the synagogue to share with them the good news of the coming of Messiah, the Jews not only rejected the message but violently abused the messengers. In turning to the Gentiles Paul was fulfilling his calling as an Apostle to the Gentiles but he was nevertheless tearing away the line of continuity with the prophets of Israel which he himself had seen as an essential element in God's plan of salvation of the whole of humanity.

III. The Nature of God

The third consequence of the Hellenisation of the church was the loss of the Hebraic understanding of the nature of God that came from the prophets of Israel. The revelation of the nature of God through the prophets, which has been the central theme of this book, gave something of unique value to the covenant people of Israel. For them it was to be shared with the entire world. This was certainly Paul's understanding which was embodied in his vision of the New Testament church being 'one new man'. The opposition to the gospel encountered among the Jewish Diaspora frustrated the achievement of this objective.

The Gentiles were much more ready to accept the gospel than were the Jews with the inevitable consequence that the churches outside Israel rapidly became Gentile institutions. In Judea, where many thousands of Jews accepted the messianic message

---

[10] see Isaiah 49.6

including *"a large number of priests"* who *"became obedient to the faith"*,[11] the church continued to expand until the Bar Kochba Revolution of AD 135. But these assemblies would have been almost exclusively Jewish, so the vision of the 'one new man' was no more relevant here than in predominantly Gentile areas of the Empire.

The Romans savagely repressed the Bar Kochba Revolution slaughtering some half a million Jews in Judaea and banning them from the land which was renamed 'Palestine' – 'land of the Philistines' as a deliberate insult to the Jews. The City of Jerusalem was utterly destroyed and renamed 'Capitolina'. Without even the Church of Jerusalem or messianic congregations in Judaea to preserve the Hebraic roots of the faith the Gentile congregations across the Mediterranean world were left adrift to develop their own traditions.

Many of the most influential Christian leaders of this period, such as Tertullian, were lawyers by profession and well versed in Latin law that had its roots in the Republic where the penal code was dominated by distributive justice, ensuring that every offender was punished in accordance with the offence. Latin legalism increasingly influenced the Gentile churches' understanding of the nature of God which paved the way for the penal substitution theory of the cross whereby Jesus' death was to satisfy the wrath of God.

This legal influence became adopted into Christianity in what became known as theological nomism [12]. But nomism was not simply a system governing standards of action, it also influenced the thinking of people in many different disciplines of life. Luther's 'third use of the law',[13] provided the rules for life not only for the Puritans and the Pilgrim Fathers but also for vast numbers of Protestants who tried to live according to what the churches taught as 'biblical standards'. Latin or Western philosophy and theology both assumed that since we live in a law-ordered universe, the law must form the basis for all social and cultural systems as well as philosophical systems.

Underlying Western Christianity, both Catholic and Protestant, is a law-based theology which is not only responsible for creating

---

[11] see Acts 6.7

[12] 'nomos' being the Greek for 'law'

[13] referred to in Chapter 11 page 179

closed minds but also for promoting intolerance. In the pre-Reformation period Latin concepts of law were highly influential in the formation and development of Christian theology. Since the Reformation the situation has been reversed and Protestant theology has been highly influential in the development of Western society and legal systems. This has been shown in numerous sociological studies beginning with Max Weber's groundbreaking thesis, 'The Protestant Ethic and the Spirit of Capitalism'.[14]

The Reformation did so much to bring the Bible into the lives of ordinary people and to break the famine of the word of God that had been there since the institutionalisation of the Early Church. Nevertheless, the Reformation was in some sense more a child of the Renaissance than of a desire to rediscover biblical truth. The Protestant Reformation did not go back to Hebraic roots to develop its biblical theology but to Latin law.

The Roman Church had already adopted Anselm's penal substitution form of theological nomism. The Reformers affirmed the same interpretation of the atonement. They re-examined Paul's teaching on justification by faith but failed to understand the Hebraic background to Paul's theology. Thus penal substitution became an acceptable doctrine in both the Catholic and the Protestant churches. This institutionalised a distorted view of the nature of God as a harsh legalist demanding full satisfaction in the punishment of sinners including his own Son.

IV. Replacement Theology

The fourth consequence of the Hellenisation of the Early Church led to 'replacement theology' which resulted from the failure of the Bar Kochba Revolution. The Jews no longer had the protection of the Emperor for their worship and they increasingly became regarded as a pariah people scattered across the Empire with no homeland and no political institution to protect their security. This also affected the Christian churches, which, up until this time, had enjoyed a certain amount of status and protection within the Roman Empire due to their association with Judaism and being regarded as a Jewish sect. The severance of the churches from Judaism had theological as well as social outcomes. It was God's intention to open the covenant to the Gentiles so that they

---

[14] Max Weber, **The Protestant Ethic and the Spirit of Capitalism** (translated by T Parsons), Allen and Unwin, London, 1977

could share with Israel in the promises and blessings. It was never his intention to blot Israel out of his promises.

The fact that God is a covenant keeping God who never breaks his promises was an essential part of the revelation of the nature of God given through the prophets. The New Covenant, prophesied in Jeremiah 31, was not given to the Gentile church. It was given to the house of Israel and the house of Judah and their descendants for ever. There was, in fact, no mention of the New Covenant being extended to the Gentiles. This was a fresh revelation given later towards the end of the exile and recorded in Isaiah 42.6 and 49.6. In the promise given to Jeremiah God swore with the most solemn oath that only if the whole physical creation vanished from his sight would he reject *"all the descendants of Israel because of all they have done"*.

Jeremiah 31.37

The loss of the church in Jerusalem and Hebrew congregations in the Galilee and Judea meant that by the middle of the Second Century the Church throughout the Empire was largely a Gentile institution with no formal links with Judaism. The churches simply took over the New Covenant promises and this paved the way for the view that the Gentile church had replaced Israel in the purposes of God. This 'replacement theology', despite it being directly contrary to the solemn promises of God given in Jeremiah 31, is still widely accepted in many parts of the church today especially among clergy and pastors who rarely read the Old Testament and even more rarely study or preach on the message of the prophets.

V. Anti-Semitism

The fifth consequence of the Hellenisation of the church and the loss of Hebraic roots was seen in the rise of anti-Semitism which had strong connections with 'replacement theology'. Anti-Semitism in Western nations, often subtle and fiercely denied, is an inherent part of European culture which is one of the outcomes of the separation of Christianity from its Hebraic roots. This separation, which was already becoming evident in the strains between Jew and Gentile in the Church in Rome in Paul's day, became institutionalised throughout the Roman Empire following the conversion of Constantine in AD 316.

The Reformation, instead of correcting this, actually increased the separation of Christianity from its Hebraic biblical roots through anti-Jewish pronouncements by Luther which strongly influenced socio/political policy in Europe. Luther's advice to the German princes of his day is acknowledged to be one of the influences behind Hitler's hatred of Jews and the Nazi Holocaust. Richard Gade in *A Historical Survey of Anti-Semitism* wrote –

"In his **'Concerning the Jews and their Lies'** Luther advised his followers to eradicate Jewish homes and synagogues by burning them to the ground and covering the site with dirt; prayer books and Talmuds were to be destroyed, rabbis silenced on pain of death, travel forbidden, wealth seized, and usury stopped; young Jews were to be enslaved at hard tasks. As a final step, Luther advocated expulsion: "Let us drive them out of the country for all time." He concluded, "To sum up, dear princes and nobles who have Jews in your domains, if this advice of mine does not suit you, then find a better one so that you and we may all be free of this insufferable devilish burden - the Jews." [15]

Of course, we cannot lay at Luther's door the whole burden of responsibility for the rise of anti-Semitism in the Western nations over the past 400 years or so. He was no doubt expressing the social attitudes of his day but the fact that he did not counter them, even by an appeal to Paul's teaching that in Christ Jew and Gentile are one, was a serious theological failure. It would, no doubt, have been a factor in the failure of the Protestant churches to take a firm stand on this issue which may also have had a bearing upon the subsequent tragic history of Europe. If we do not get our theology right it has far-reaching social consequences!

VI. God as Unbreakable Love

The sixth, and arguably the most serious, consequence of the Hellenisation of the church is to be seen in the loss of the biblical revelation of the nature of God as unbreakable love.

It is important to note that the biblical revelation of God does not just speak of God's love as a quality that he offers to us human beings. Rather, it speaks of 'love' being an essential element in the nature of God. It is an attribute of his being, not just something he offers – as we would offer to do a kindness to a friend. The New Testament says that God actually *IS love!* [16]

---

[15] Richard E Gade, **A Historical Survey of Anti-Semitism**, Baker Book House, Grand Rapids, 1981, p.51

This revelation, first given to the prophets of Israel and developed in the person and work of Jesus, is central to a right understanding of the promises of God, his purposes, and the way in which he intends working out those purposes and fulfilling his promises. This places a huge burden of responsibility upon Christian leaders to ensure that their theology is soundly rooted in biblical revelation and to ensure that they are rightly expressing the word of God and not simply reflecting human philosophies and social values.

The history of Christianity in the past one thousand years has been more associated with violent action than promoting forebearance, understanding and peacemaking. If the church had got its theology [17] right this could never have happened. The drive to establish the Kingdom of God on earth by conquest has no foundation in the New Testament yet this was an objective of the Crusades. Jesus specifically said that his Kingdom is not of this world otherwise his followers would fight. His teaching in the Sermon on the Mount is unambiguous;

"Do not resist an evil person. If someone strikes you on the right cheek, turn to him the other also." Matthew 5.39 Even more strong was the command, *"Love your enemies and pray for those who persecute you".*   Matthew 5.44

Following the Reformation, conflict and war between different branches of the Christian Church in the West became a regular feature of life in different parts of Europe. This violence was not simply between Roman Catholics and Protestants, but between Protestant and Protestant in what today we would consider trivial doctrinal disputes. In 1525, Zwingli, the Swiss Reformer, launched a violent campaign against Anabaptists. In 1536 Melanchthon went a step farther issuing a memorandum demanding the death of Anabaptists.

In neither of these disputes did Luther intervene to cool tempers or to urge tolerance. Similarly, Calvin did not intervene in Geneva when Servetus was taken to the stake in a doctrinal dispute. Servetus was offered a reprieve if he would confess that Jesus was 'the Eternal Son of God'. He replied, "I confess that Jesus is the Son of the Eternal God." But that was not sufficient for these strict Protestant theologians, and self-appointed guardians of the

---

[16] 1 John 4.8

[17] by 'theology' is meant 'teaching on the nature of God'

faith. They condemned Servetus to suffer the incredible agonies of being burned in a slow fire. When he finally fell down into the flames his dying words were, "O Jesus, thou Son of the Eternal God, have pity on me!"

The infamous Spanish Inquisition that began around 1478 was initially aimed primarily at Jews in an attempt to counter their influence upon Catholic Christians. This was further evidence of the growing divide between Hebraic biblical scholarship and Western Christianity. Some historians estimate that there were 2,000 victims burned at the stake during the first 10 years. The Inquisition did not exclusively persecute Jews but it also included Protestants (although these were few in number) and Muslims. The numerous trials with associated torture were to ensure that converts had thoroughly renounced their former religious practices and were adhering to the Catholic Church. It is variously estimated that the number of executions carried out by the Inquisition during the period 1560 to 1700 was between 3,000 and 5,000.

Religious violence among Christians is by no means a thing of the past. Acts of violence are still carried out by extremists on the fringe of Christianity although they are not representative of mainstream Christian thought. The troubles in Northern Ireland that brought death and destruction into the lives of many hundreds of Catholics and Protestants have still not been finally settled and violence permanently repudiated.

Nevertheless, mainline Christian churches have been committed to policies of peace and tolerance since the latter half of the 19th century which in part has been due to the increasing influence of liberal theology. Sadly, it is true to say that the triumph of tolerance in civil law has been gained, in most Western nations, not so much through the campaigning of devout Christians, as through the work of secularists, humanists and political campaigners.

New Biblical Reformation

In light of the record of Western nations where the majority of their populations claim to be Christians, the history of bloodshed and violence stands in sharp contrast to the teaching of the New Testament and especially to the witness of Jesus. Clearly there has been a failure to communicate biblical theology into the social and political institutions where national policies are formulated. The church has singularly failed to communicate the revelation of the nature of God as unbreakable love and his requirements that those who are brought into a right relationship with himself through Christ show the same quality of love.

Clearly, there is a need for a new Biblical Reformation that does not simply look at church traditions but goes back to biblical roots and examines the revelation given to the prophets and is developed in the New Testament.

Such a Biblical Reformation, uncovering the Hebrew roots of the Christian faith that were entrusted to the Early Church, would also have a radical effect upon our theological concept of the nature of God. It could produce a transformational movement of social, moral and ethical change in society as the unbreakable love of God becomes translated into public policy.

Index

WORD REFERENCE

BIBLICAL REFERENCE

Unbreakable *Love*